Day Tripping:

Kayak Wisconsin

Door County Peninsula

Bluffs, Beaches, Lighthouses, and Shipwrecks

Babs Smith

Book cover photo:
Deaths Door, paddling towards Table Bluff

Back cover photo
Varney Point Newport State Park

Kayak Wisconsin, Door County Peninsula

Photos by:
Babs Malchow Smith
Rick and Chris Malchow
Becky Malchow Jeske
Michael Smith

Graphic Design:
Ryan Malchow
Mark Malco

A portion of the cost of this book is donated to the Door County Land Trust

Copyright © 2014 Babs Smith
All rights reserved.
ISBN: 0692433880
ISBN-13: 978-0692433881

Bluffs, Beaches, Lighthouses and Shipwrecks

CONTENTS

	Our Adventure begins	Pg i
	Safety and Stuff	Pg iii
Leg 1	**Go Pack Go!** Green Bay to University of Green Bay- Lambeau Cottage *with Bay Beach Amusement Park* 4 miles	Pg 1
Leg 2	**The Real Green Bay** University of Green Bay to Bay Shore County Park *with Point au Sable Nature Preserve, and Point Comfort* 11.5 miles	Pg 11
Leg 3	**Into Door County** Bay Shore County Park to Chaudoir's Dock County Park *with Red River Park* 10 miles	Pg 21
Leg 4	**Sugar Creek** Chaudoir's Dock County Park to Sugar Creek County Park *with the beginnings of the Niagara Escarpment high bluffs* 4 miles	Pg 31

Kayak Wisconsin, Door County Peninsula

| Leg 5 | **Niagara Escarpment** Sugar Creek County Park to Little Sturgeon Bay | Pg 39 |

with Lime Kiln ruins, a shipwreck, and Caflin & Carmody County Parks

9 miles

| Leg 6 | **Potawatomi** Little Sturgeon Bay to Potawatomi State Park on Sturgeon Bay | Pg 49 |

with Sand Bay Beach, Cliff Drive Beach and the Sherwood Point Lighthouse

9 miles

| Leg 7 | **Sturgeon Bay** Potawatomi State Park through Sturgeon Bay & channel to Lake Michigan | Pg 61 |

with Olde Stone Quarry Park, shipbuilding in progress, two lighthouses, and lots of shipwrecks

10 miles

| Leg 8 | **Olde Stone Quarry** Olde Stone Quarry County Park to Frank Murphy County Park | Pg 79 |

with Pebble Beach, Lady Slipper, and Sunset Lanes

9 miles

| Leg 9 | **Tour the Towns** Frank Murphy County Park to Peninsula State Park | Pg 91 |

with Egg Harbor, Fish Creek: the towns, the beaches, the sunsets

11.5 miles

Bluffs, Beaches, Lighthouses and Shipwrecks

Leg 10	**Sister Islands**
	Peninsula Park to Porcupine Bay Road
	    with Sister Islands OR
	    Ephraim and Sister Bay and Bluffs
	10 miles
		Pg
		105

Leg 11	**Tip of Door's thumb**
	Sister Bay at Porcupine Bay Road to Garret Bay
	    with Ellison Bay and Bluff,
	    Deathdoor Bluff, and a sunken ship
	6 miles
		Pg
		117

Leg 12	**Deaths Door**
	Garret Bay in Hedgehog Harbor to Europe Bay Lake Michigan
	    with Gills Rock, Table Bluff,
	    views of Washington Island
	    and Newport State Park
	7 miles
		Pg
		127

Leg 13	**The Wilderness**
	Europe Bay to Mink River Estuary and Rowleys Bay
	    with nature lover's Newport State
	    Park and the Mink River Estuary
	10 miles
		Pg
		139

Leg 14	**The Wild Side**
	Rowleys Bay to North Bay
	    with North Bay Natural Area and
	    Sand Bay Beach and
	    two century old shipwrecks
	9 miles
		Pg
		149

Leg 15	**Lighthouses**
	North Bay to Baileys Harbor
	    with Cana Island Lighthouse,
	    and Baileys Harbor Lighthouse
	10.5 miles
		Pg
		159

Contents

Kayak Wisconsin, Door County Peninsula

Leg 16	**Cave Point** Baileys Harbor to Jacksonport to Whitefish Dunes State Park *with Cave Point's caves, sand dunes and beaches at Whitefish Bay, and lots of shipwrecks* 11 miles	Pg 175
Leg 17	**Dunes & Shipwrecks** Whitefish Dunes State Park to Lily Bay *with the tallest sand dunes, sandy beaches, and fun shipwrecks* 10 miles	Pg 187
Leg 18	**Beaches** Lily Bay Beach to Salona Road Beach *with Lake Lane beach and Lake Michigan Drive beaches, and the Sturgeon Bay Lighthouses* 6 miles	Pg 199
Leg 19	**High Banks** Salona Road Beach to Algoma *with lost ghost towns, lost shipwrecks, and a beautiful tri-level shoreline* 11.5 miles	Pg 213
Leg 20	**Sandy Bluffs** Algoma to Kewaunee *with the scenic sandy bluffs, the iconic Lighthouses and two beautiful creeks* 12 miles	Pg 227

Bluffs, Beaches, Lighthouses and Shipwrecks

Isle	**Crossing Deaths Door** Circle tour Northport to Plum Island, Pilot Island, and Detroit Island *with Plum Island range lights and shipwreck, Pilot Island's lighthouse, and Detroit Island* 11.5 miles	Pg 241
Isle	**Washington Island Lakeside** Ferry Dock access to Jackson Harbor Ridges Park *with Gislason, Sand Dunes, and Percy Park Beaches, & shipwrecks* 11 miles	Pg 255
Isle	**Washington Island Bayside Bluffs** Jackson Harbor Ridges Park to Ferry Dock access *with Schoolhouse Beach and shipwreck, and Little Lake* 14 miles	Pg 271
Isle	**Rock Island Naturally** Great Circumferential Paddle *with an expansive sand beach, sheer bluffs, and historic stone buildings* 9 miles	Pg 287
Isle	**Chambers and the Strawberry Islands** Peninsula State Park through the Strawberry Islands to Chambers Island *with Chambers Island Lighthouse and an expansive view of the bluffs of Door County* 12 miles	Pg 301
	About the Author	Pg 315

Kayak Wisconsin, Door County Peninsula

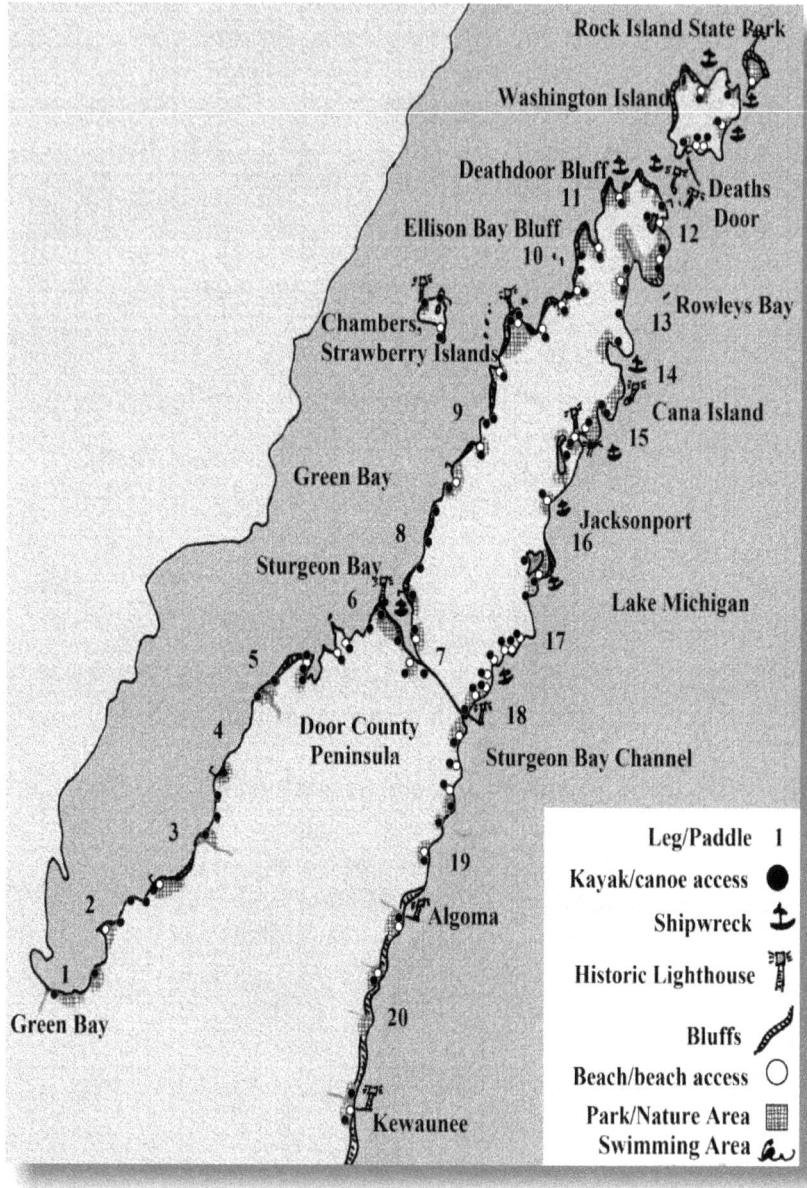

Bluffs, Beaches, Lighthouses and Shipwrecks

Our Adventure Begins

Our Adventure begins years ago when we started kayaking, originally in recreational kayaks, but the Lake Michigan and of course, Green Bay, called us. Rick and Chris bought sea kayaks, and persuaded me to join in. We started with little jaunts from Suamico to Long Tail Point and played on the beach. We realized what all the yachts and sailboats have known for years—Green Bay is a boater's paradise!

Trips to the Apostle Islands, and Pictured Rocks all on Lake Superior followed. All very awesome! But why not explore closer to home—basically our own backyard in northeast Wisconsin? Hence our decision, circumnavigate around the Door County Peninsula. We are real folks, with real jobs—not professional athletes or extreme sporters in anyway.

So we decided to paddle completely around Wisconsin's Door Peninsula in realistic day trips—that other regular folks who like to kayak can do also. Rick and Chris, and I, Rick's sister, have accomplished our endeavor—not even in one year, but in several years. Lots of family and friends have joined us for portions of this adventure. We hope our experience helps you enjoy the incredible beauty of the Door Peninsula in Wisconsin.

Bluffs, Beaches, Lighthouses and Shipwrecks

Safety and Stuff

Sea Kayaks: To paddle in Green Bay and especially on the Lake Michigan side of Door County, we highly recommend sea kayaks or at least "transitional kayaks". They are longer and slimmer than recreation kayaks, with more maneuverability and hatch space. We are not purists, our kayaks have rudders to help us steer, some of us use the rudder most of the time, some only when tired or the water is a bit rough.

A PFD: Personal Floatation Device: better known as a lifejacket. We recommend you wear it all the time, as the weather may have different plans than you have. . . .Or at least keep it in very close range, such as immediately behind you for easy access for when the waves and wind decide to fool you.

A good paddle: doesn't matter if you use a traditional blade or a Greenland blade, ergonomic or straight, but your paddle should be light (so you don't get as sore and tired). Floatable is helpful as a sinking paddle is not much help. . . Recommend that your paddle not be metal. Rick says that dropping your paddle on your lap every time there is lightening in a storm where you are at a brick wall (OK not brick, but solid rock) is not helpful, I think it has to be better than having the blade look an awful lot like a lightning rod!

Know and practice rescues: During an emergency is NOT the time to try to figure out or remember how to do a rescue. There are classes you can take, such as at the Door County Symposium held every summer, or your local YMCA may offer classes. Then practice at least one time a year, more often is obviously better, and can be a lot of fun too—especially on a hot summer day.

Kayak skirt: needed on any of the Great Lakes. Wear the skirt—if it starts out nice, you can have one that zips down to keep cool, but can zip up if the weather rises up. Please don't keep your skirt in your hatches, they are just not accessible when needed.

Rick's 3 essentials: We now carry safety gear at all times. This includes Rick's 3 essentials:

 A flashlight: preferably LED, it's amazing how many times you stop and play and end up pulling the kayak's out in the dark, Rick also swears by a headband light so two hands are free.

A lighter: in case safety dictates a fire and very nice for HOT food! If you are a klutz, like me, then you could switch to matches instead, just keep them in a dry bag.

Bluffs, Beaches, Lighthouses and Shipwrecks

And a pocket knife: you never know when you'll need it, and you tend to need it a lot more than you expect.

You can always color coordinate the 3 essentials to your boat color as Rick does. He always has his 3 essentials in his pocket, never sure which pocket, but always in his least likely pocket.

Plan ahead and know the weather: Rick is our "weather man". He researches the forecast the day before, day of, and then we all listen to the emergency radio's forecast on shore before embarking. Even then we have been surprised by a change in the wind direction, strength of the wind, or storms that suddenly decide to blow in.

Kayak Wisconsin, Door County Peninsula

One nice thing about paddling Door County is that there is always a lee side! This book is arranged in serial legs starting in Green Bay and doing the bay side, around the tip, and then the lake side. But don't plan to do it that order. Listen to the weather and choose the side that will be the "lee" or quiet side, unless of course you love waves crashing over you, then by all means choose the wild side! Generally, the Lake Michigan side of the peninsula is the more wild side in summer, and going around the tip is called going through "Death's door". Many shipwrecks have happened there, so plan that leg carefully.

Food: Dry food in case you can't make it back to where you started (because of said weather changes—mother nature likes to keep us guessing you know). You can always land, hunker down and eat. Eating is nice and when using up energy paddling, you tend to do a lot of it.

Water: more than you think you will need. And a water pump that can change questionable water into drinking water and/or tablets that can also do that if your water pump dies on the trip, been there, done that.

A tarp: We have found by cold experience that kayak skirts do NOT make a good umbrella (they do have a hole in them you know), so we now always have at least one tarp. Dry is always a plus if a storm suddenly pops up.

Dry clothes in a dry bag: Dry clothes are always better if they stay dry! If you tip over or roll, the rest of the trip can be agonizingly cold, better to land and switch to dry clothes. Fleece or the old time favorite wool (much of which is now not so itchy) keeps you warm even when wet.
Bring a fleece or wool blanket for the same reason also. Spending a night cold makes for a very long night.

Wet suit: Many experienced kayakers never venture onto Lake Michigan without wearing a wet suit, it's your call.
Toilet paper: Every trip needs that, works as Kleenex (tissue if you are not from Wisconsin) in a pinch too.

First aid kit: Ours keeps growing every time we wish we had something. Our first aid kit includes aspirin/ibroprofin, band aids for little hurts, bandages and tape for bigger hurts, coban wrap– better known in Wisconsin as "vet wrap" available at farm stores, which substitutes for tape or splints if needed, and holds band aids on better for blisters on hands. Chris always has her bee sting rescue pen (which thank God we have not needed yet–knock on wood), I carry Benadryl Itch stopping cream (after a discovery that I am allergic to "no see' em" when camping on an island), and Rick has a tennis elbow splint (in case that decides to flare up). Then you might as long bring along an Icy Hot gel which does seem to help relieve achy muscles.

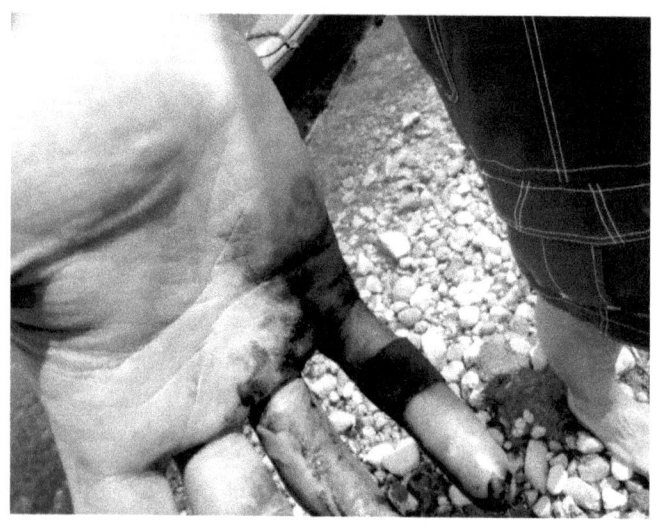

A white night light: that attaches onto the back deck of your kayak when it starts getting dark, 'cause you played so long in the surf! Kind of a legal thing too. . . Based on Coast Guard regulations: "a vessel under 7 meters (23 feet) must have at hand a white electric torch or lantern which shall be exhibited in sufficient time to prevent a collision from sunset to sunrise." Best if you keep your light in an accessible place (i.e.: not in your hatches) because you can't always find a good place to land when it starts getting dark.

A GPS: waterproof and made for boating, and extra batteries, not much help when it clunks out. It is amazing how many arguments we have had over where we are and where is that take out spot—sure looks different from the water than when standing on shore. . .

A flare to alert rescue help: If something bad does happen, it would be helpful to have a rescue team find you. An emergency radio would be helpful too, not cheap, but it allows you to send a signal for help if needed.

Anything we missed? Not trying to scare you, but paddling should be fun and not a life threatening experience. So knowing what you are doing and how you would handle issues helps keep it fun.

Oh yeah, and wine. . .or at least we like one little glass when we stop on the beautiful shore.

Kayak Wisconsin, Door County Peninsula

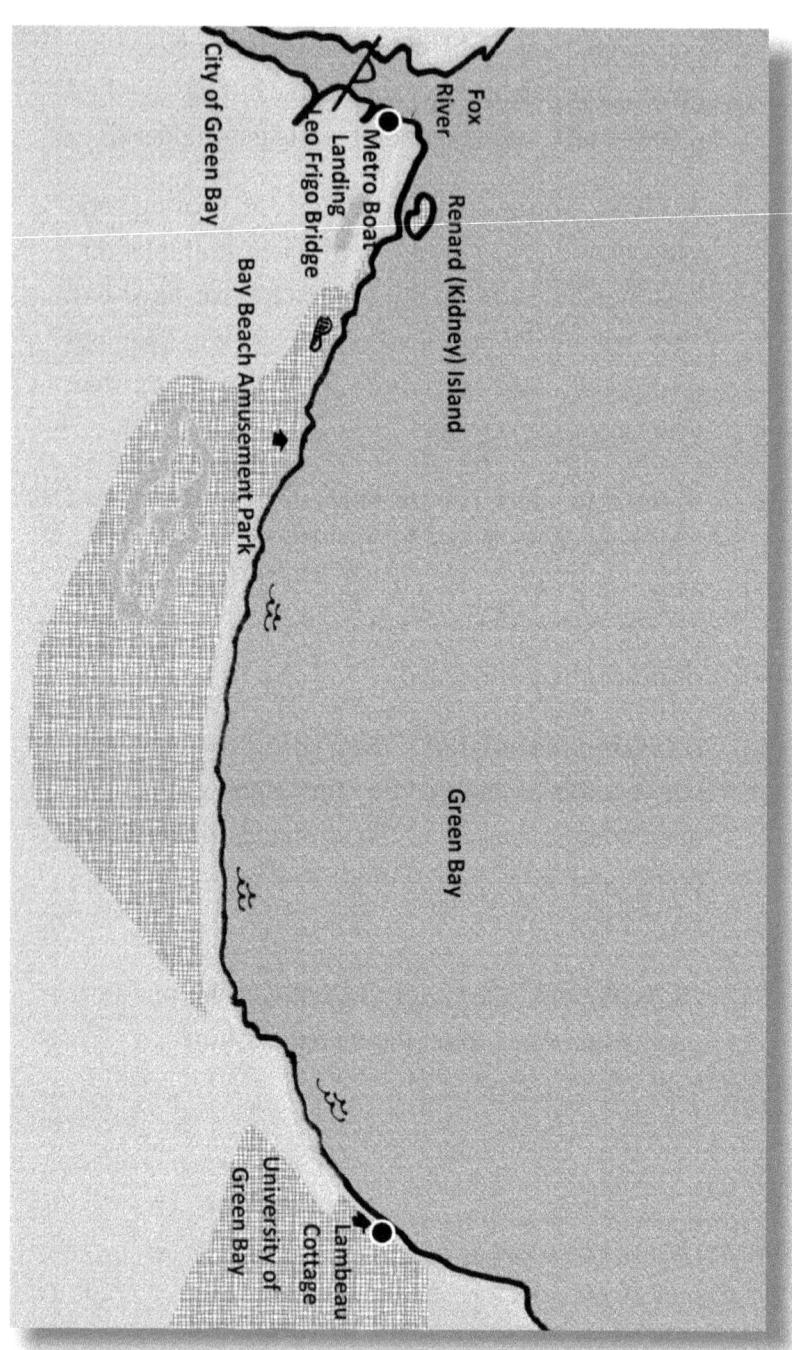

Leg 1

Go Pack Go!

Green Bay Metro boat landing to Lambeau Cottage at UW Green Bay

With Bay Beach Amusement Park
4 miles

Go Pack Go! Our initial official start to our circumnavigating Wisconsin's Door Peninsula, starts in "Titletown"—the world famous city of Green Bay and cruises past the Bay Beach Amusement Park with the Zippin Pippin, a roller coaster Elvis Presley used to ride, and the University of Wisconsin—Green Bay's peaceful shoreline and ends at Curly Lambeau's, the famous Packer coach, real cottage.

Interested in a longer paddle? Add some ruralness to the paddle by putting in at Duck Creek off the end of West Deerfield Ave and paddle to the south end of the little lagoon, through the small channel and follow Duck Creek to the bay of Green Bay then head east to Wisconsin's Door Peninsula. Otherwise add some urbaness to your paddle by asking permission from Zellers Sport Shop to use their private boat landing in Green Bay. Better yet, stop in and buy some gear or snacks for your day! The Fox River in the city of Green Bay is an ultra nice urban paddle. From Zeller's boat landing, paddle north "down" the river as it is one of the few rivers that actually flow north. Float under some beautiful downtown bridges to the bay of Green Bay and again head east to Wisconsin's Door Peninsula. Urban versus rural, either paddle is awesome and would add on about 3 miles and give you a wonderful view of the towering Leo Frigo Bridge.

Yeah, we are missing the Packer game. Honestly we are good fans, even owners, not many folks can say they are owners of a national team, but we can. No true Packer fan would rather paddle than watch the game, right? Choices, choices, Packer game versus paddling? Ah, relaxing paddling—they don't know what they are missing. But in our defense, it is a beautiful autumn day, and paddling is so much easier on the nerves than a close Packer game (and they always seem to be close). Relaxing paddling. . .just tell us they won–Yeah! Cheer!

We put in at "Bay Beach", the city of Green Bay's Metro Boat landing with the wonderful view of Green Bay's Leo Frigo Tower Drive Bridge which soars high above the river to allow big ships into the port of the city of Green Bay. All

Bluffs, Beaches, Lighthouses and Shipwrecks

those cars missing out on this, come on down and enjoy the bay Green Bay is actually named after. Wow what a gem Green Bay has! Come down to the beginning of Wisconsin's peninsula and enjoy the water.

The city of Green Bay is located in the crux of the bay of Green Bay, at the base of the peninsula between the thumb and the main land mass of Wisconsin. Green Bay is Wisconsin's oldest city, the third largest in Wisconsin, and the smallest city in the country to have its own National Football team, the Packers, just in case you haven't heard of them. The Packers are the only team to be owned by its fans and has so many national championships, that the city of Green Bay is known as "Titletown". Green Bay has a really fun Packer Hall of Fame, its own beautiful riverwalk, and of course is situated on the amazing bay of Green Bay!

We choose to head out of the Fox River, into the bay of Green Bay and turn right, northeast, that's the direction to follow the Door Peninsula. Wisconsin's "big thumb" is part of the Niagara escarpment—yup, that's right—the same cliff that the Niagara Fall tumbles over. The Peninsula is in Lake Michigan and divides the lake and forms the huge bay of Green Bay. The bay is the largest freshwater estuary in the world and is 120 miles

Kayak Wisconsin, Door County Peninsula

long and averages 23 miles wide and has its own wind and wave action. Green Bay is 10,000 years old, formed when the glaciers receded.

The Door Peninsula that separates Green Bay from Lake Michigan tapers northeastward to its tip. At the top of the "thumb" is the strait between Green Bay and Lake Michigan known as Death's Door because this is where the waters of Green Bay collide with the waters of Lake Michigan creating a dangerous passage that is littered with shipwrecks.

As we start our adventure towards Death's Door and head northeast away from the city of Green Bay, along the bay of Green Bay's coast of its peninsula, we already see an island. Named Kidney Island (because of its shape) or Renard Isle comes into view. This is a manmade island, has nesting bird colonies and is planned as recreation area and wildlife habitat.

We glide by the Zippin Pippin roller coaster at Bay Beach Amusement Park. It is a great place for taking the kids in summer—there is no admission charge, parking is free and rides costs a quarter to fifty cents, except the new Zippin Pippin which costs one whole dollar. OK, OK, the Zippin Pippin isn't really new, it was bought from Memphis Tennessee, and it is said that Elvis

Bluffs, Beaches, Lighthouses and Shipwrecks

Presley used to ride it, so you could actually be sitting in the same seat Elvis did.

Go past the beautiful Bay Beach historical columned pavilion, maybe even land and stop in for a quick peek. Dating from the 1930's the pavilion was an attraction for concerts, political rallies, dances, fireworks, and President Franklin D. Roosevelt even visited it in 1934 in celebration of Green Bay's tercentennial.

Paddling offers lots of time for contemplation as we settle into the gentle paddle, quiet, peacefulness right by the city. Most folks have put away their boats for the season. The whole Green Bay, just for us! We can look over to Long Tail Island on Wisconsin's mainland. Long

Kayak Wisconsin, Door County Peninsula

Tail "island" is really a peninsula, but you can only get to it by boat. It shimmers across the lower end of the west side of the bay. South of Long Tail, is Dead Horse Bay, wanna guess why it is called that? Our ancestors who lived on the shore of the little bay, used to harvest blocks of ice from the frozen bay for pre refrigerator ice boxes, and back then they used horses to pull the ice wagons, and lost a few horses when they went through the ice. Thankfully, the advent of the refrigerator caused the demise of the ice harvesting business and the risk to horses.

We paddle up to the Green Bay campus, and stop for a stretch at, of course, Lambeau's Cottage! Curly Lambeau was the Packer's first coach for an unheard of 28 years and had 6 NFL championships. He is the legend that the Packer's stadium is named for and the famous "Lambeau Leap" completed after each home game touchdown. OK, so we're not home watching the game, but we are "in spirit" with the Packers (Go Pack Go!). Sit on a big warm rock and eat cheese (see, we really are Cheeseheads) and crackers and drinking good old Wisconsin beer, wait. . .it was actually wine, aw shucks we goofed that one up.

Looking out over the sparkling bay, life doesn't get much better than this and it is in northeast

Wisconsin. Lake Michigan and Green Bay is just as awesome as an ocean without sharks, alligators or jellyfish. Yup, just give us this beach right here in our home state.

Taking a sip, Rick stands up and says "Some people spend good money for this", Chris replies "and we did too", and I respond, pointing out at the bay, "but not as much as that yacht".

Logistics:

Directions to the city of Green Bay's Metro Boat landing:

44.5383, -88.0027. 102 Bay Beach Road, Green Bay WI (west of Bay Beach Amusement Park):

I-43 to East Shore Drive/N. Webster Ave. (Exit 187), east on East Shore Dr, turn left on Irwin Ave. Irwin Ave. will turn into Bay Beach Rd. at the entrance of Bay Beach Amusement Park. Follow Bay Beach Rd. west to Metro Boat Launch. Fee to launch, but there are restrooms.

Kayak Wisconsin, Door County Peninsula

Directions to Lambeau Cottage on the University of Green Bay:

44.5353, -87.9299. 2479 Nicolet Drive, Green Bay WI. Highway 54/57 north towards Sturgeon Bay exit on Nicolet Drive and go north. Lambeau Cottage and parking lot is off of Nicolet Drive on the University of Green Bay. You will need to carry boats over a few rocks to the shoreline. No fees, no restrooms.

Directions to Bay Beach Amusement Park:

44.5313, -87.9786. 1313 Bay Beach Road, Green Bay WI. I-43 to East Shore Drive/N. Webster Ave. (Exit 187), turn east on East Shore Dr, then left onto N. Irwin Ave, turn right into parking lot for Bay Beach Amusement Park.

Directions to Duck Creek for a longer rural paddle:

44.5676, -88.0495. 1100 W. Deerfield Ave, Green Bay WI. From Hwy 41/141 exit Lineville Road, travel south on West Deerfield Avenue 2 miles to its end at Duck Creek.

Directions to Zellers Ski and Sport Shop and private boat ramp:

44.4982, -88.0219. 1212 Marine St, Green Bay WI. From Hwy 41 exit on 172 East. Go over the Fox River and exit Riverside Drive. Drive north on Riverside/Monroe Ave for 2 miles and turn left on Marine Street. Go down the hill and at the T intersection turn right to Zellers Ski and Sport Shop and their private boat ramp.

Kayak Wisconsin, Door County Peninsula

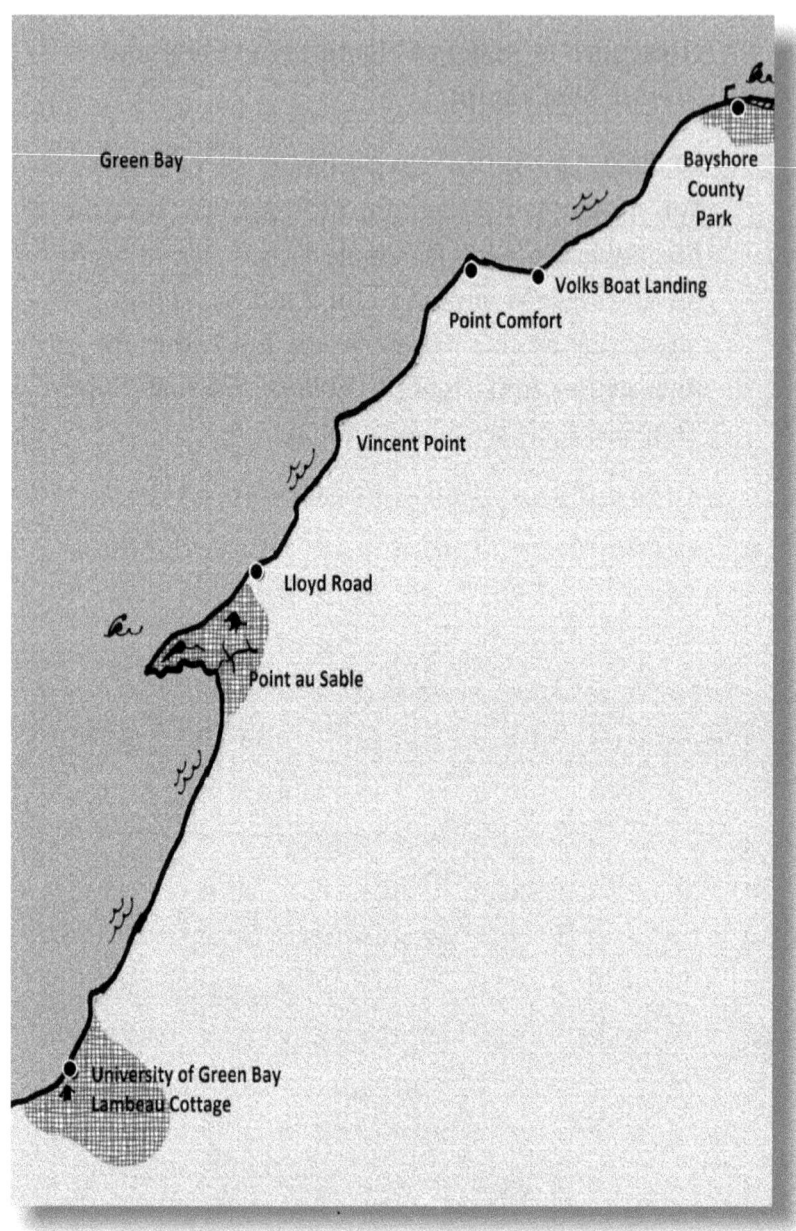

Bluffs, Beaches, Lighthouses and Shipwrecks

Leg 2:

The Real Green Bay

Lambeau Cottage at UW Green Bay to Bayshore County Park

With Point au Sable Nature Preserve, and Point Comfort
10.5 miles

On Wisconsin, On Wisconsin! Okay, just on the big bountiful bay of Green Bay. Our second leg of the Door Peninsula tours the only accessible by boat Point au Sable nature preserve saved just for "the birds", along with Point Comfort, Edgewater beach and ends at Bayshore County Park with its beautiful bluffs and swimming beach.

Yes, this paddle is a teensy bit more than 10 miles. Point Comfort has a small public access at the end of Point Comfort Road to divide this paddle into a 6 mile and then a 4 mile paddle from Point Comfort to Bayshore County Park. Volk's landing is another public access point about 2 miles south of Bayshore County Park and could be your take out spot to decrease the length of this paddle to about 8 miles. It is just a small road off of Edgewater Beach Road down to the shoreline.

Kayak Wisconsin, Door County Peninsula

With no dock or restroom, Volk's Boat Landing is generally only used by small craft, which would make it a quieter take out spot than Bayshore Park.

Launched at Lambeau Cottage, the same spot of leg 1's take out, that way you can be sure you haven't missed even one foot of shoreline. The University of Green Bay is a very pretty campus, with an arboretum that circles the campus with miles of hiking trails through forests, prairies, wetlands, limestone bluffs and of course the half mile of shoreline. Just north of Lambeau Cottage is Communiversity beach, cute name huh! You can launch a canoe or kayak anywhere along the stretch of the bay between Lambeau Cottage and Communiversity beach at the University of Green Bay as there is no formal boat landing and public access is encouraged. For this day trip, we used two cars and parked one at Bayshore County Park boat landing as the "chase" car.

Was a beautiful and warm autumn day when we launched at Lambeau Cottage and quiet since most of the boaters had already put their boats in storage. They really missed a great day. The bay was calm and peaceful, a wonderful day to explore nature at its best.

Bluffs, Beaches, Lighthouses and Shipwrecks

We took an early break and stopped for a snack at the first point, Point au Sauble, one of the few big public areas on this day trip. Point au Sauble is a nature reserve that is only accessible by boat. Wequiock Creek ends up here after the spectacular Wequiock Falls pours over the Niagara Escarpment east of Point au Sable. Previously Point au Sable was a private duck hunting camp and no public roads have ever been built on the point. The last of the private duck hunters donated the point as a nature preserve just "for the birds" forever. And it is a great place for birds as it is one of largest wetland areas on the whole west side of the Door Peninsula! Thousands of migratory waterfowl pass through this area on their way south. Go ahead and hike

the trails to search this wonderful nature center saved for us and the birds. Point au Sable has one of the highest densities of woodpeckers, or search for the elusive marsh dwelling Least Bittern. We took the opportunity to stretch our legs after paddling and enjoyed watching the shorebirds. Notice the terns with their gray wings, forked tails, black caps and orange bills with a black tip, as they plunge from the air to the water to catch their fish. Watch the slim and trim great egret stand sentinel waiting for its prey to come close enough to spear with his long sharp bill. As the egret stands stark still, he shows off his four foot height with long legs, neck and bill. When he does fly off, he showcases his five foot wingspan. Enjoy the flocks of American White Pelicans flying in. They have chosen to make the Green Bay and Door Peninsula their new nesting area. With their 16 pounds, they are one of the largest birds in North America and have the second longest wingspan of up to nine stunning feet! They are joy to watch fly with their long bill and extensible pouch, short legs, webbed feet, and their crooked Z tucked neck when the glide through the air.

The water is very shallow and clear all along the Point au Sable area and you could get out and swim at any point. Justin, a newbie, kind of did

Bluffs, Beaches, Lighthouses and Shipwrecks

as he decided to get to know his kayak and how far he could lean before going over. Not that far, and no, you can't use the water to push yourself back up. But luckily for him, it is so shallow, that you can push up off the bottom and only get a little wet!

A short distance past Point au Sauble, there is a public access spot off of Lloyd Road that could be used to launch kayaks. The next little point is Vincent Point and then you see Comfort Point, not sure why it is called this, we like to think that someone needed to take comfort in a storm at this little point, or did a couple get a little too cozy one day? Point Comfort Road does have a public access at the end of the road with a short path to the beach. If you planned for a shorter paddle, this would be your take out spot.

The rest of the paddle is along Edgewater Beach and is generally nice homes and cottages to goggle at and guess at the selling prices. If I was rich, I'd buy that one, no wait, that one's even nicer. . .Nice sandy beach front, but not conducive to stopping and relaxing or swimming, unless your kayak has a small anchor. . .

Being November, the days are shorter and even shorter than normal if you forget about Daylight Savings time ending. We had to stop for a short break to get out our white night lights for the boats, and then finished our paddle by moonlight. Moonlight paddles on Green Bay are a wonderful experience as the water often calms down and the moon sparkles off the water. We stopped at Volk's boat landing, a small public access area off of Edgewater Beach Road down to the shoreline. It does have a small parking area, with a small bench and a port-a-potty. This would be a nice quiet take out spot rather than Bayshore County Park.

However, we continued onto our planned take out spot at Bayshore County Park and tonight's moonlit paddle is in November and the night is a bit chilly. We see the light, we see the light! Go to the light! The light is calling us, yeah it really is, it is the parking lot light of Bayshore Park. By this time, it is a welcome relief, especially for Justin who was wet and pretty cold by now. Always end the trip with a paddle lift high above the head!

When coming from the south, go out and around Bayshore's stone break wall and enter the marina from the north side. We continued past the marina and landed on the sandy beach. But there are some rocks that you need to carry the boats over to get to the parking lot.

Bluffs, Beaches, Lighthouses and Shipwrecks

As we pull up the boats, Rick takes the chase car to retrieve the other car at the launch site. Thankfully, we do have Rick's "3 essentials" lighter, pocket knife and most importantly tonight—flashlights! Appreciate that Rick encouraged us to buy headband LED lights, perfect for hands free loading of the vehicles. The boat landing and beach does have a nice restroom, so you don't have to find a tree to go behind. Also helpful when wet and cold, right Justin?

The moonlight flickers off the bluff, our first real view of the Niagara Escarpment as we circumnavigate around Wisconsin's Door Peninsula. Our flashlights glint off the high ledge, giving us an eerily quiet view of the of the 400 million year old geologic formation created by an ancient sea. A dramatic dazzling scene as we explore the real bay of Green Bay.

Logistics:

Directions to Lambeau Cottage on the University of Green Bay:

44.5353, -87.9299. 2479 Nicolet Drive, Green Bay. Highway 54/57 north towards Sturgeon Bay exit on Nicolet Drive and go north. Lambeau Cottage and parking lot is off of Nicolet Drive on the University of Green Bay. You will need to carry boats over a few rocks to the shoreline. No fees, no restrooms.

Directions to Lloyd Road public access:

44.5877, -87.8942. From Highway 57 turn west on Highway K. Highway K ends at County Road A/Nicolet Drive, turn right/north on County Road A. Turn left at the first road, Point Lane and then turn right onto Lloyd Road and follow it to the bay. No fees, no restrooms.

Directions to Point Comfort Road public access:

44.6190, -87.8551. 4899 Point Comfort Road. From Highway 57 turn onto County Road A (Nicolet Drive) towards the bay, turn right onto Point Comfort Road and follow it until it dead ends at the public access site on Green Bay. No fees, no restrooms.

Bluffs, Beaches, Lighthouses and Shipwrecks

Directions to Volks Boat Landing:

44.6186, -87.8431. 4699 Volks Landing Road. Take County Road A west towards the bay off of Highway 57, almost immediately take the first right on Sturgeon Bay Road, then left on Stone Pillar Road, right on Edgewater Beach Road and look for Volks Landing Road, the short road to the parking area for Volks boat landing. No fees but there are restrooms!

Directions to Bayshore County Park:

44.6379, -87.8030. 5637 Sturgeon Bay Rd. New Franken. Heading north on Highway 57, turn left onto Gravel Pit Road, then immediately right on Sturgeon Bay Road to park, turn left at fork in road—continuing on Sturgeon Bay Road and go down the hill to the boat landing. Fee to launch and there are restrooms

Kayak Wisconsin, Door County Peninsula

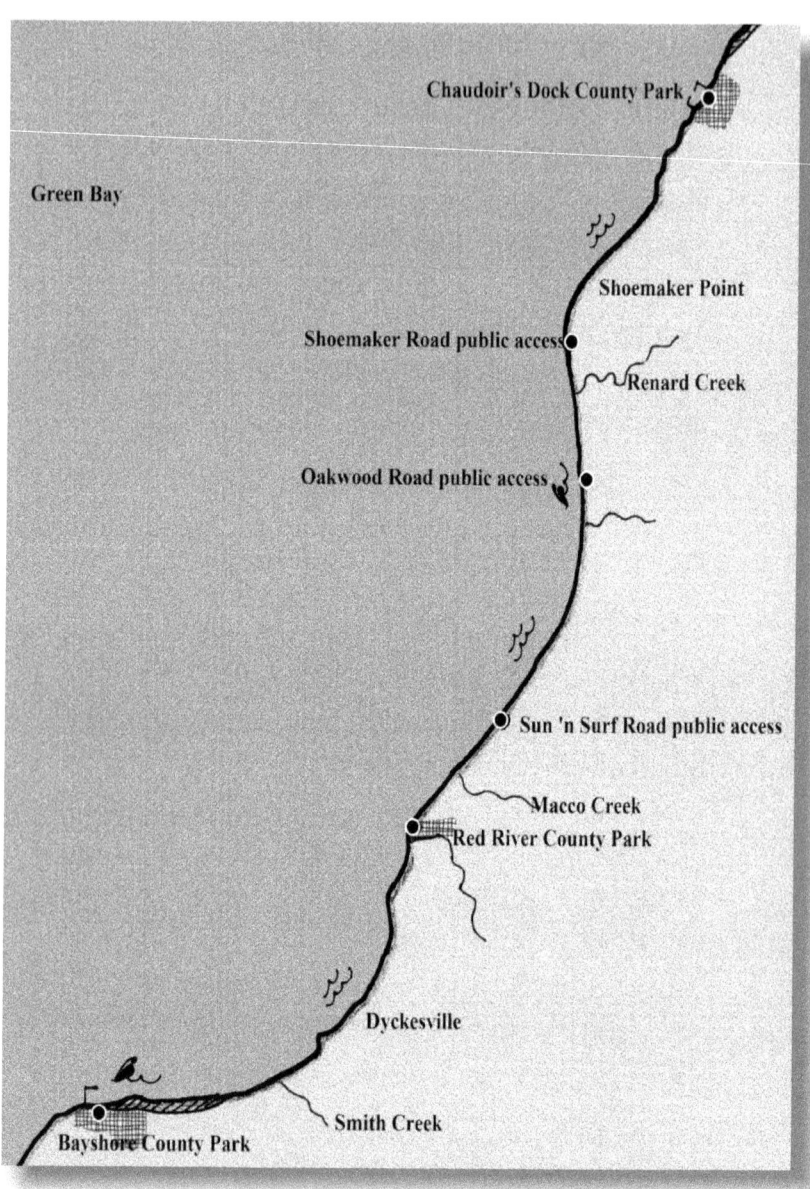

Bluffs, Beaches, Lighthouses and Shipwrecks

Leg 3:

Into Door County

Bayshore County Park to Chaudoir's Dock County Park

With Red River Park
10 miles

1-2 Life is good, 3-4 into the Door. This paddle tours several beautiful often missed County Parks starting at Bayshore, cruising past Red River and ending at Chaudoir's Dock County Park. We are already entering Door County!

Want a shorter trip? To cut this day trip in half, use the Red River County Park. This park is located two miles north of Dyckesville on State Hwy. 57, and has picnic tables, grills, shelters and restrooms, always appreciated! Kayaking from Bayshore County Park to Red River is approximately 5 miles, and then Red River to Chaudoir's Dock is about 5 miles.

Launched at Bayshore County Park, this time in summer. This park can get very busy, and it may be easiest staying to the right in the parking lot and carry boats over the rocks to the beach to launch, rather than use the boat landing. Stop and dive in for a quick swim prior to launching as it has a great 2000 foot long sandy beach. The full name of the park is the Cecil Depeau Bay Shore County Park. Not sure who he is, but sure was nice of him to share this park and kayak launch with us. The boat ramp is down the hill to the water's edge. But look up and notice the Niagara Escarpment as it already begins. It was created by an ancient sea 400 million years ago, a little before our time. . . The park has nice trails that follow the ledge and lead down to the beach. Bayshore's water's edge attracts migrating songbirds, shorebirds and waterfowl. There is even an old lime kiln to view 600 feet south of the break wall. The park is known for its awesome nautical themed playground. You can even camp here and enjoy the sunset as you relax around your campfire.

Cousin Ben joined us for this leg. His roots are in Wisconsin as our heritage farm is located in Suamico, always fun to share the day with family and friends. He has jumped into kayaking with great memories of canoeing as a child with his Dad.

As we start our third leg paddling north up the Door Peninsula, we float past the small Smith Creek and then the small town of Dyckesville in a shallow bay. About a half mile north of Smith Creek, float up onto the shore in Dyckesville for

Lipsky's on the bay Restaurant, known for fire baked pizza, hamburgers and fresh perch.

Then up towards little Barrett's Point. For these few minutes we are actually in a corner of Kewaunee County. The name "Kewaunee" is one of many Native American names in Wisconsin—this one is Potowatomi for "we are lost", it is said that people lost in fog offshore would call out "Kewaunee, Kewaunee" to be guided safely to shore from answering calls on land. However, today, for us, it was a pure blue sky with no hint of fog, perfect for kayaking.

Kayak Wisconsin, Door County Peninsula

About five miles into our paddle, we discover Red River County Park. The Red "river" actually is a stream with intermittent flows, sometimes a river, sometimes a creek the meanders through meadow and shrub over bedrock until it reaches Green Bay and this nice County Park known mostly by fisherman. We had lunch on the delightful mouth of the river with its small sandy beach strewn with boulders. There was a colony of pelicans lounging just off shore by a transitory island. These American White Pelicans, once scarce to Wisconsin, have taken to Wisconsin's Door Peninsula, like Packer fans have to cheese hats. Pelicans are hefty fellows with orange bills and feet and are just a delight to paddle past and to share our beach with. They can live up to thirty years, so we'll see them back each year. The Red River Park certainly would be an easy kayak launch with its gentle beach sprinkled with purple, yellow and white wildflowers.

After the Red River, paddle past Sun'n Surf road which does have a small public access point you could stop or launch at, then breeze past Breezy Acres, Beauty View Court, and Sandbar Lane (don't they all sound so pleasant?) as you leave Kewaunee County and paddle into Door County itself. Between Breezy Acres and Beauty View Court there is a public access point at the end of

Bluffs, Beaches, Lighthouses and Shipwrecks

Cedar Road. We paddle past arrowhead and sandbar beach, and discover another small public access at the end of Oakwood Road for you to enjoy the beach too. Perhaps it is time for another swim?

On this trip we are enchanted by  the beautiful bald eagles watching us glide by. Eagles are fairly common now in Wisconsin and along the peninsula. Eagles prefer large trees with a close proximity to areas of open waters. Duh, no wonder the eagles have chosen Green Bay's shoreline. They eat mostly fish which they catch by swooping down and snatching with their talons. Bald eagles build the largest nests of any North American bird up to 6 feet wide and 3 feet deep. They have up to 7 foot wingspan and weigh up to 14 pounds with the females bigger than males–you go girl! The Bald Eagle has rightly been the national emblem of the US since 1782 and a spiritual symbol for Wisconsin's native people as they are majestic birds with their white head plumage as they soar without flapping their wings. Our eagles seem amused by us as we try to glide silently past them.

Other common birds along the bay include ducks, egrets, warblers, thrushes, tern, and gulls. The Door is also home to deer, wild turkeys, and yes, even an occasional wolf and black bear, oh my!

We wave goodbye to our eagles and look north to Shoemaker Point. It is a fairly large point. Tried to visualize it as a shoe, but it just doesn't really look like one at all, maybe it is suppose to look like the shoemaker? We paddle pass Renard Creek before the tip of the point. Renard Creek runs and riffles through woods and meadows as it zigzags its way to Green Bay. At the tip of Shoemaker Point at the end of Shoemaker Road there is another small public access area.

Enjoy the shore of the bay as we round the point, and we head to Chaudoir's Dock. You will see the protective harbor walls of Chaudoir's Dock as you approach it. North of the protective harbor is an area that is best suited to launching and taking out kayaks, and the parking lot is nearby. There are navigation lights in case you arrive after dark.

Bluffs, Beaches, Lighthouses and Shipwrecks

Logistics:

Directions to Bayshore County Park:

44.6378, -87.8030. 5637 Sturgeon Bay Rd. New Franken. Heading north on Highway 57, turn left onto Gravel Pit Road, then immediately right on Sturgeon Bay Road to park, turn left at fork in road—continuing on Sturgeon Bay Road and go down the hill to the boat landing. This park also has 150 campsites with showers, laundry, and electricity. The boat landing and beach area does have nice restrooms, but they can get busy also! Fee for launching.

Directions to Red River County Park:

44.6683, -87.7475. This park is 2 miles north of Dyckesville. From Hwy 57 take County Road X west towards the bay, then a quick right onto DK, after .7 miles turn left on Park Road. No fee, but there are restrooms.

Kayak Wisconsin, Door County Peninsula

Directions to Sun 'n Surf Road public access:

44.6796, -87.7327. From Highway 57 exit on W. County Line Road/Sun 'n Surf Road towards the bay and follow Sun n' Surf Road to the bay! No fee, but no restrooms either.

Directions to Cedar Road public access:

44.6914, -87.7209. From Highway 57 exit on Sun 'n Surf Road towards the bay and immediately turn north on County DK and drive about 1 mile to Cedar Road and follow it to the bay. No fee, no restrooms.

Directions to Oakwood Road public access:

44.7059, -87.7184. From Highway 57 exit on D towards bay, then immediate left on County Road DK, then a right on Oakwood Road and follow it to the bay! No fee, but no restrooms either.

Bluffs, Beaches, Lighthouses and Shipwrecks

Directions to Shoemaker Road public access:

44.7206, -87.7215. From Highway 57 exit on D towards bay, then immediate left on County Road DK, then right on Stage Road and another right onto Shoemaker Road and follow it to the bay! No fees, but no restrooms either.

Directions to Chaudoir Dock County Park:

44.7467, -87.6982. 1552 County N in the Town of Union. From Hwy 57 turn onto County Road D west towards the bay and then an immediate right onto DK, followed by a first left onto Pleasant Ridge Road for 1.3 miles, then turn left onto County Road N, there will be a right, then left, and then another right turn as you follow N to Chaudoirs Dock. The Park has a protective harbor and dock on Green Bay and facilities include a boat launch, picnic area, parking and restrooms. Fee for launching.

Kayak Wisconsin, Door County Peninsula

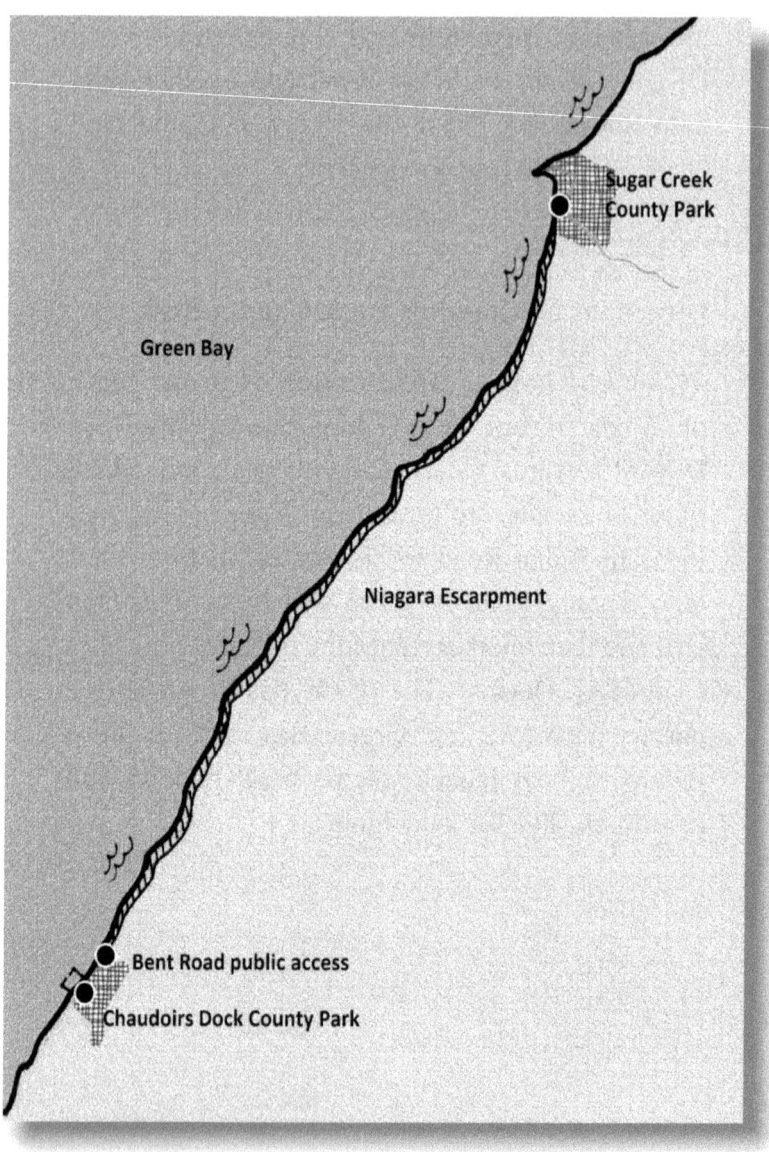

Bluffs, Beaches, Lighthouses and Shipwrecks

Leg 4:

Sugar Creek

Chaudoir's Dock County Park to Sugar Creek County Park

With the beginnings of the Niagara Escarpment high bluffs
4 miles

Sugar, sugar, you've got me wanting you. Leg 4 has lots of beautiful bluffs above the shoreline and ends at the scenic Sugar Creek County Park. With such a nice quick paddle, Leg 4 leaves you with time to explore inner Door County and cherries galore.

Yup, it's a short paddle, but you could add this paddle onto the previous leg and paddle from Bayshore County Park to Sugar Creek for a 13 mile paddle. But consider doing the short paddle and giving yourself some extra time to enjoy the bay view from Sugar Creek County Park. It would be awesome to plan this paddle in the late afternoon and then enjoy the sunset from Sugar Creek Park.

This short paddle gives you time, take the time to check out the Door County cherries. If you plan this paddle for late spring then you can enjoy the

Kayak Wisconsin, Door County Peninsula

famous cherry blossoms, or if you choose late summer, then it is harvest time, and eating time! There are cherry stands nearby to buy a quart or two. But we swear they taste even better if you climb the ladders yourself. We prefer the sweet cherries, but the deeper the red pigment, the better the health benefits. Door County Cherries are America's Super fruit, so delicious and so healthy. Door County tart cherries are full of antioxidants and are anti-inflammatory; they can reduce arthritis and gout pain, lower risk factors for heart disease by lowering cholesterol and triglycerides along with body weight and fat, reduce diabetes risk, and decrease insomnia. And best for us, it may decrease post exercise pain, so eat up! Buy fresh sweet or tart cherries, dried cherries, frozen cherries, cherry jam, cherry jelly, cherries covered in dark chocolate. . . and cherry salsa—a jar is a must. Yum, yum.

OK, onward with paddling. We put in at Chaudoir's Dock, best to avoid all the motor boat traffic and put in north of the protective harbor on the beach. There is a parking lot nearby. Chaudoir's Dock is a favorite picnic spot with picnic tables and grills. The beach has 625 feet of shoreline to enjoy and just a little north of the beach is Bent Road public access. This may actually be a quieter spot to launch your kayaks.

Bluffs, Beaches, Lighthouses and Shipwrecks

It's a calm day for paddling along a shore that seems to get prettier as you go north along the coast of Door County. Lots of green, visitors from out of state always comment on of how "green" and pretty Wisconsin is, and when you place that against the aqua blue of the bay, it is a gorgeous place to be! On such a calm, warm, summer day it is easy to get lulled into the rhythm of the paddle and enjoy the warmth of the sun.

Stay close to the shore and you could be surprised by Door County's diversity of wildflowers interspersed in the greenery. In spring search for primrose, the rare dwarf iris, the beautiful white lacy bog buckbean or the little purple miniature

airplane looking gaywing. If you are paddling in summer than you could spy one of Door County's twenty-five native orchids including the yellow lady slipper, yellow coreopsis, or the bright orange lilium wood lily on whorled leaved stems.

Point your bow towards the small point on the horizon and enjoy the bluffs as we paddle north. The cliffs you see are part of the Niagara Escarpment that start in New York by Niagara Falls, follows the Lake Ontario southern shoreline, through Lake Huron creating Georgian Bay and then curves around the top of Lake Michigan, down into the Door Peninsula, and even continues into mainland Wisconsin and forms the eastern shoreline of Lake Winnebago. 'Gotta admit, it's pretty spectacular work by Mother Nature.

Since this is just a petite little paddle, perhaps it is time to slow down and check out some fishing on the bay. Yup you can do that from a kayak. Popular fishing includes walleye, perch, northern, bass, crappies, brown trout, and even muskies—but maybe not those from the kayak as you might go for a fast ride behind a big fish!

Sugar Creek County Park has a pretty little bay to glide into. It is a mostly wooded park that is popular with smelt-dippers, netting another of

Bluffs, Beaches, Lighthouses and Shipwrecks

Green Bay's fish. There are picnic spots and a nice clean outhouse at the north end of the parking lot behind a few trees. It is generally a quiet park mostly used by kayaks and other small watercraft. Sugar Creek really is a stream that meanders through lower Door County wetlands and cobblestones and empties into Green Bay at the park.

Sugar Creek's mini bay is a nice place to swim although it is not designated as a beach. Once you get past the shoreline it has a great sandy bottom, with a quiet spot to swim and relax in the bay. We also took some time to explore and hiked a

short way to the mouth of Sugar Creek. Since this is a quick paddle, bring your Frisbee golf discs because Sugar Creek now has a new 18 hole disc golf course. Pack up the kayaks and let's just enjoy some disc'n on gentle rolling terrain in old growth hardwoods entwined by the creek.

After kayaking, cherry picking, and disc golfing, go ahead and sit above the Sugar Creek escarpment and take pleasure in the view especially famous for sunsets. Enjoy this unheralded gem of a Door County Park!

Logistics:

Directions to Chaudoir's Dock County Park:

44.7467, -87.6982. 1552 County N in the Town of Union. From Hwy 57 turn onto County Road D west towards the bay and then an immediate right onto DK, followed by the first left onto Pleasant Ridge Road for 1.3 miles, then turn left onto County Road N, there will be a right, then left, and then another right turn as you follow N to Chaudoir's Dock. The Park has a protective harbor and dock on Green Bay and facilities include a boat launch, picnic area, parking and restrooms. There is a launch fee.

Directions to Bent Road public access:

44.7487, -87.6961. From Hwy 57 turn onto County Road D west towards the bay and then an immediate right onto DK, followed by the first left onto Pleasant Ridge Road for 1.3 miles, then turn left onto County Road N, there will be a right, then left, and then another right turn as you follow N to Chaudoir's Dock Road. Continue past Chaudoir's Dock County Park to where the road turns left. This is Bent Road and turn right to the dead end for the public access spot.

Directions to Sugar Creek County Park:

44.7867, -87.6609. From Highway 57 turn north on County Road C, turn left on 4 Corners Road (the one after Lovers Lane—isn't that cute!), 4 Corners Road turns into County N, then turn right into Sugar Creek County Park. Go down the hill to the parking lot and boat landing. There are some picnic tables and a nice outhouse located at the north end of the parking lot. There is a launch fee box.

Kayak Wisconsin, Door County Peninsula

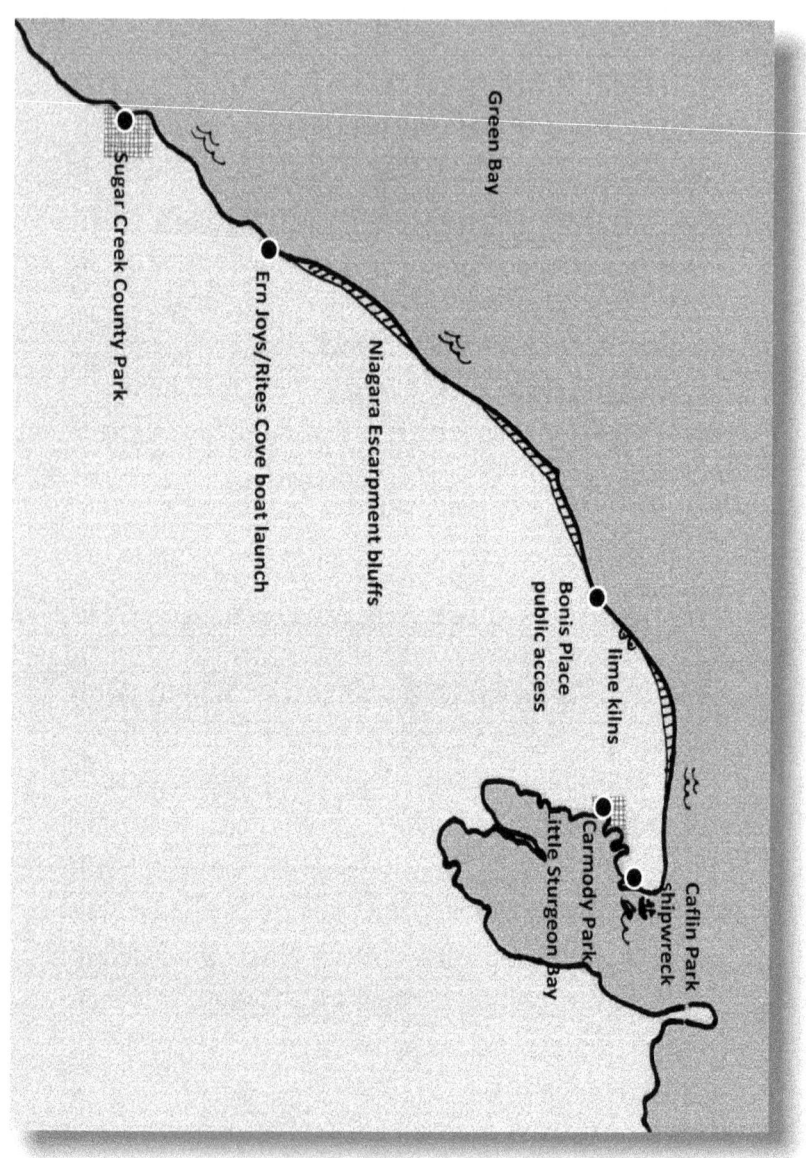

38

Leg 5

Niagara Escarpment

Sugar Creek County Park to Little Sturgeon Bay

With Lime Kiln ruins, a shipwreck, and Claflin and Robert Carmody County Parks
9 miles

New York! New York! Wait, no, no this is Wisconsin. But we are talking about the Niagara Falls Bluff that curves all the way from New York to form the western edge of the Door Peninsula. This is a great and fun paddle trip that includes some great views of the twenty plus foot cliffs, a lime kiln ruins, Little Sturgeon Bay and our first possible shipwreck sighting.

Because of the high cliffs, there is no halfway point to access, unless you want to pitch your kayak off the cliff. . . You could decrease the distance at the beginning by launching at Ern-Joys (now Rites Cove) boat ramp at the end of Gravel Pit Road (County N that turns into Wilcox Road or Bay Road depending on which map you are using) for a 7 ½ mile paddle, or shorten the paddle by kayaking from Sugar Creek County Park to

Kayak Wisconsin, Door County Peninsula

Bonis Place public access, before Little Sturgeon Bay Point, for a 6 mile paddle.

We launched at Sugar Creek County Park with no crowds at the boat landing and the gorgeous view of the bay from the top of the Niagara Escarpment. Stop and enjoy. Maybe even swim. Load up the kayaks, check the weather forecast one more time. . .couldn't be better. . .great sunny, summer day, with very few clouds–where's the sun screen, where's the hat?

Off we start, and very quickly the cliffs begin to grow and the scenery becomes stunning. The Niagara Escarpment ridge is formed by gently tilted sedimentary rock strata with the rock edges exposed on the bluff, so lucky for us! It is called a cuesta because it has a gradual slope on one side—the eastern shore of the Door Peninsula and Lake Michigan and the dramatic cliff on the other side, the western Door Peninsula bluff shoreline on Green Bay. This is one of the unique natural wonders of the world that was created 440 million years ago just for us to marvel at today.

Take time, relax, rhythm, repeat, just an awesome day to enjoy summer in Wisconsin. We glide past Ern-Joys public access spot, just a dead end road access popular with fisherman and in the winter snowmobiles. It is called Ern-Joys after a bar that

Kayak Wisconsin, Door County Peninsula

used to be there, now the bar is called Rites Cove, and it is hard to miss as they have HUGE Adirondack chairs by water's edge. Stop in for a beverage and enjoy the view from their little patio. The road is Bay Road or Wilcox Road or County N or Gravel Pit Road at its eastern end, take your pick, the maps all seem to.

Justin, the son-in-law to be, and newbie from Leg 2 has joined us for this trip. He has taken to kayaking like a sea otter to a rock slide and can out kayak the best of us in a recreation kayak. His male elder also taught him how to ram Aunt Babs' kayak and make her turn this way, and then that way. . .great fun for the young 'uns.

By Bonis Place, a public access spot, we stop under the cliffs for a fabulous lunch by Chef Rick and his propane stove. Great things can be cooked on a tiny stove by the walls of a mighty

Bluffs, Beaches, Lighthouses and Shipwrecks

cliff. Sit on the rocks, and breathe great clean air with an awesome view, both to the cliff and out to the bay. Sip some water, sway to the rhythm of the lapping of the waves on the rocks. A picturesque spot for a break and after lunch we wade on in, slipping and sliding on the wet rocks, and swim and play for wonderful summer splash.

Once our appetites are satiated and our swim is complete, we are ready to hop back into the kayaks and travel on. More and more lovely views–watch for the old Lime Kiln ruins on the shoreline. You could stop on such a calm day to investigate the ruins, however we chose to glide past enjoying the interesting lime kilns from our boats.

Now we begin to round about Henderson Point and paddle into Little Sturgeon Bay. The town of Little Sturgeon was known for its shipbuilding and there is actually a shipwreck at Claflin County Park. The wreck is about 850 feet south around the little point of Claflin's Memorial Rock, close to shore in Little Sturgeon Bay, and goes out to a depth of about 15 feet.

The park is named after Increase Claflin, the first permanent white settler in Door County. Look to the middle of Little Sturgeon Bay and you see the long thin line of Squaw Point jutting out, during

Kayak Wisconsin, Door County Peninsula

Increase Claflin's time there was a village of 500 Menominee natives that lived there that Claflin traded with.

Claflin Park would be a quiet take out spot for kayaks, but we chose to continue onto Robert Carmody County Park. It is easy to find as it is next to the Wave Pointe Resort. The Wave Pointe has its own private marina. We have enjoyed staying there for our winter get a ways and have enjoyed our suites with nice warm cozy cuddly fireplaces along with incredible views. At Carmody County Park, you will have to use one of the six boat launch ramps for taking out the kayaks as there is a large rock pile next to the boat launches. You could stop and fish here as the pier extends out nearly 200 feet into Little Sturgeon Bay.

While Rick chased for the other car, we considered jumping the fence to swim in the resort pool–awfully inviting after a warm paddle–but probably illegal, so we chose to swim off the rocks next to the boat launches. Probably not the best idea as Justin suddenly scooted out of the water dripping blood from a wound on his hand. Chris and I brought out the first aid kit and high fived each other as this was the first time we ever needed to use the first aid kit for anything besides the usual aches and pains. Justin was a little worried at that point about marrying into this family... But Robert Carmody County Park has nice restrooms with running water to clean such wounds and to change out of wet swimsuits. Lesson learned.

Logistics:

Directions to Sugar Creek County Park:

44.7867, -87.6609. From Highway 57 turn north on County Road C, turn left on 4 Corners Road (the one after Lovers Lane—awh!), 4 Corners Road turns into County N, then turn right into Sugar Creek County Park. Go down the hill to the parking lot and boat landing. There are some picnic tables and a nice outhouse located at the north end of the parking lot, fee for launching.

Directions to Ern-Joys Public access:

44.8032, -87.6427. From Highway 57 turn north on County Road C, go about 5 ½ miles on C and turn left on County N/Gravel Pit Road, follow this approximately 1 mile to where it dead ends at the bay. No fee, but also no restrooms. But Rites

Kayak Wisconsin, Door County Peninsula

Cove Bar is right there, stop in for a beverage, enjoy the view and the big chairs by water's edge and use the restrooms there.

Directions to Bonis Place public access:

44.8431, -87.5934. From Highways 57 turn north on County Road C, go approximately 6 ½ miles and turn right and continue to follow County Road C another 1 ¼ miles and then turn north onto Lime Kiln Road for about 1 ½ miles and keep going straight onto Bonis Place when Lime Kiln Road turns to the right. There is a small parking area, no fee but also no restrooms.

Directions to Claflin County Park:

44.8479, -87.5515. In case you prefer to take out your small craft at a more quiet, secluded park, then use Claflin County Park. From Highway 57 at Brussels, take County Road C north towards the bay, turn right and continue following C, turn left onto County Road CC, past Robert Carmody County Park, turn right onto Claflin Road (where County Road C ends), follow Claflin Road until it runs into Little Sturgeon Bay. No fee, no rest rooms.

Bluffs, Beaches, Lighthouses and Shipwrecks

Directions to Robert Carmody County Park:

44.8440, -87.5598. 3570 County Road CC on the west shore of Little Sturgeon Bay. From Highway 57 at Brussels, take County Road C north towards the bay, turn right and continue following C, turn left onto County Road CC, the park and boat landing is on your right just before the big resort. There are nice restrooms and picnic tables and grills available, fee to launch.

Shipwreck Location:

Unidentified Shipwreck: 44.8460, -87.5500. Lies in Little Sturgeon Bay just 850 feet south of the point of Claflin County Park. It is close to shore in about 15 feet of water.

Kayak Wisconsin, Door County Peninsula

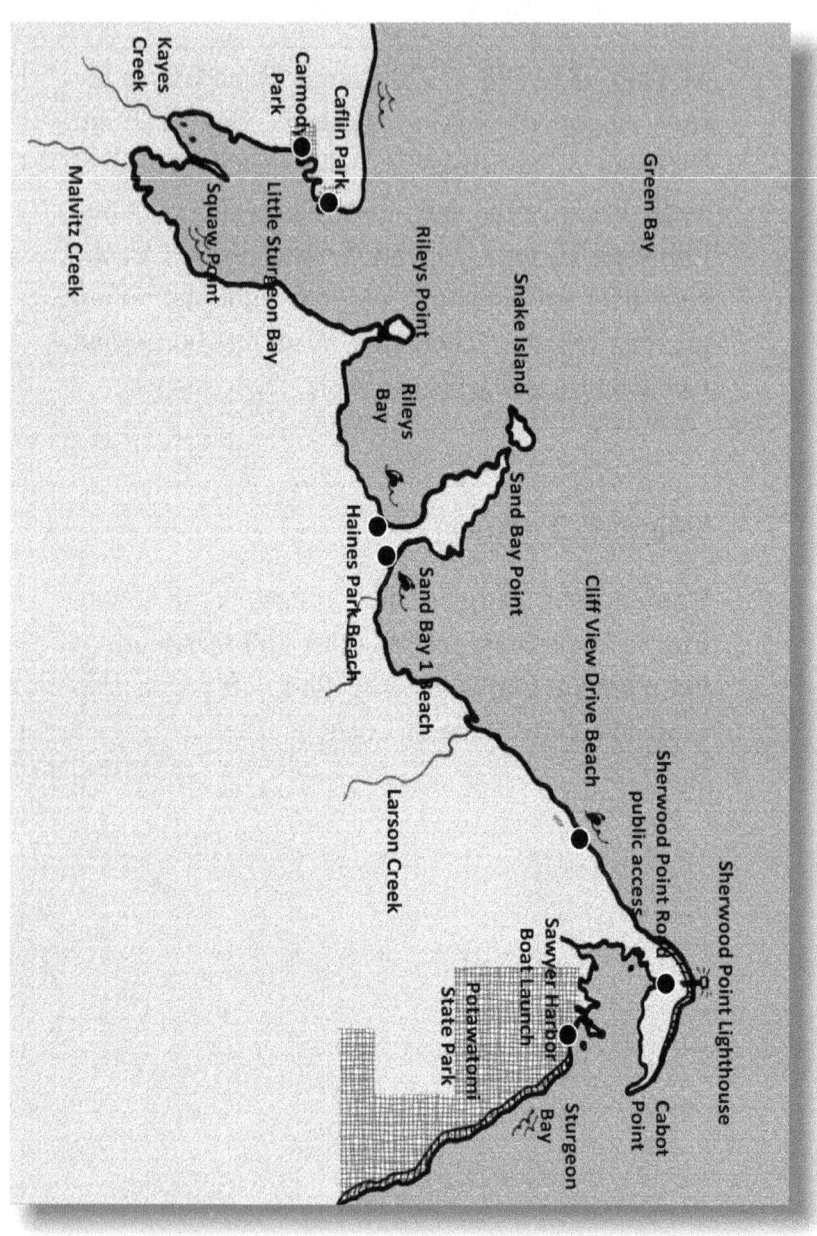

Leg 6

Potawatomi

Little Sturgeon Bay to
Potawatomi State Park on Sturgeon Bay
*With Sand Bay Beach, Cliff Drive Beach
and the Sherwood Point Lighthouse*
9 miles

Potawatomi, Potawatomi, many of Wisconsin's towns and landmarks have Native American names. Potawatomi is the name of the tribe who lived in the Door Peninsula when the French explorers first came to the Door in 1600's. The name Potawatomi means "keeper of the sacred fire". This leg of our paddle takes us through many nooks and crannies of points and Southern Door's bays, by serene beaches and then mighty cliffs from the Niagara Escarpment, our first Door County Lighthouse, and ends at one of the best state parks in Wisconsin–Potawatomi.

Take your pick of put in spot in Little Sturgeon Bay, the quieter Claflin County Park and take a chance at finding the shipwreck off the point, or the busier (but it has nice restrooms) at Robert Carmody County Park next to the Wave Pointe Resort marina. We chose to put in at our same take out spot–Robert Carmody County Park as you can't actually say you've circumnavigated Door County if you miss a single latitude or longitude.

Little Sturgeon Bay is a deep protected bay. Two little creeks, Kayes and Malvitz Creek flow into the bay after riffling through Gardner State Wildlife Area further inland. Squaw Point juts out in Little Sturgeon Bay between the two creeks and there was once a thriving Menominee Village on this point when the first white settlers found the bay. Little Sturgeon Bay is tucked away in a secluded, peaceful area known for great sport fishing including walleye, smallmouth bass, trout, pike and perch. The bay has a great laid back feeling with quiet solitude for relaxing and enjoying the views and sunsets.

From Little Sturgeon Bay we skirted past Riley's Point and swooped into Riley's Bay along the shoreline to catch Haines Park Beach located on the south side of Sand Bay. Then we aimed for Sand Bay Point and Snake Island. Want to guess if there are lots of snakes on the island or does it look like a snake as you paddle towards it? Actually, it is the largest private island in all of Door County.

We threaded the needle between Snake Island and Sand Bay Point. OK, OK, we had to stop and re

bandage Justin's hand from our leg the day before. Rick refused to get out of his kayak "this soon" but it actually was a pleasant little view.

The next bay is Sand Bay and on the north side of Sand Bay Point there is another public beach spot. Ready for another swim? Sand Bay Beach #1 is at the end of Sand Bay Lane next to the resort. The sandy beaches are so delightful that they named the whole bay after it.

Head straight for the next point, Sherwood Point, with the gorgeous cliffs. Paddle past Larson Creek that runs through meadows, shrubs and woods and then flows into Green Bay. These numerous creeks are great fisheries for the bay fish. Before you reach the point, there is another public beach at the end of Cliff View Drive. We never knew there were so many great public beach accesses in Door County.

Sherwood Point is unmistakable due to the 30 foot limestone bluffs, part of the Niagara Escarpment. Look up! The Sherwood Point lighthouse is on top! The lighthouse was built in 1883 and was the last manned lighthouse on the Great Lakes. It took one century for it to become automated, and in all that time, there were only three lighthouse keepers. The Sherwood Point lighthouse has a ten sided cast iron lantern room. Don't bother to

Bluffs, Beaches, Lighthouses and Shipwrecks

bring along your crampons, carabineers and climbing ropes, as it is closed to the public as the old keeper's house is used as a retreat for the coast guard. But you're in luck in May, as they open the doors for Door County's Lighthouse Walk Festival. The festival even offers trolley lighthouse tours and a ghost tour which includes the Sherwood Point lighthouse. Guess it must be haunted?! Guests at the lighthouse report hearing voices and walking on the stairs, and mysterious cleaning including dishes put away, dinner table being set, and beds made. The opinion is that Minnie, one of the first women light keepers in the whole country with her husband William Cochems, is still in her Lighthouse home. She collapsed and died in her bedroom in 1828. William erected a memorial birdbath for Minnie which is still located on the Lighthouse grounds.

Kayak Wisconsin, Door County Peninsula

After the historic view of the Sherwood Lighthouse with its fourth order freznel lens, go round the corner and paddle into Sturgeon Bay along Cabot Point. We landed on the rocks along the bluff and set up for lunch. An incredible vista, but perhaps we wrecked the view of the passing tour boats looking up at the lighthouse. . .

After a long play, eat, and swim time, we slid back into our kayaks and rounded Cabot Point and sailed on into Sawyer Harbor. The harbor is ringed by Potawatomi State Park on the south side of the harbor and that is where the boat landing is, kind of under the observation tower.

Sturgeon Bay is a gigantic bay that is naturally seven miles long and then the Shipping Canal was cut through the rest of it to actually make the upper half of Door County an island. The city of Sturgeon Bay is at the original end of Sturgeon Bay. Sturgeon Bay is so big that Sawyer Harbor is a little bay in the big bay.

Potawatomi is the first of the plethora of state parks that Door County has to offer as we circumnavigate around it. The park has 11 miles of trails with one leading to a 75 foot tall observation tower—need even a better vista? Guess 30 foot limestone bluffs is not quite enough of a view. There are birch lined trails atop the

Bluffs, Beaches, Lighthouses and Shipwrecks

limestone ridges which are part of the Niagara Escarpment—yes, coming all the way from the Niagara Falls! The hiking here is so important, it marks the beginning of the National Ice Age Scenic Trail. If you haven't had enough exercise yet today you could start walking the Ice Age trail as it winds for 1200 miles across Wisconsin. . . This state park is one of the best in the state and is considered one "not to be missed!"

Prefer to stay on the water? Then again you are in the right place, the protective Sawyer Harbor offers some of the best fishing in Door County—great for walleye and bass.

Potawatomi State Park does enforce the fee to enter the park. Might as well get the yearly sticker as Potawatomi is only the first of the whopping five state parks Door County offers.

If you prefer a more quiet take out spot, you can take out at the other side of Sawyer Harbor at the end of Sherwood Point Road, off of County M. It again is a road that ends at the harbor. Straight shot in, but difficult to turn around a kayak trailer.

Kayak Wisconsin, Door County Peninsula

Logistics:

Directions to Robert Carmody County Park:

44.8440, -87.5598. 3570 County Road CC on the west shore of Little Sturgeon Bay. From Highway 57 at Brussels, take County Road C north towards the bay, turn right and continue following C, at the Little Brown Jug Bar turn left onto County Road CC, the park and boat landing is on your right just before the Wave Pointe Marina and Resort. There are nice restrooms and picnic tables and grills available.

Directions to Claflin County Park:

44.8478, -87.5507. In case you prefer to launch your small craft at a more quiet secluded park, then use Claflin County Park. From Highway 57 at Brussels, take County Road C north towards the bay, turn right and continue following C, at the Little Brown Jug turn left onto County Road CC past Robert Carmody County Park, turn right onto Claflin Road (where County Road C ends), follow Claflin Road until it runs into Little Sturgeon Bay.

Bluffs, Beaches, Lighthouses and Shipwrecks

Directions to Haines Park Beach, Sand Bay Point Road:

44.8549, -87.5045. From Highway 57, turn north on Stone Road and go approximately 3 miles, turn left on Highway County C, then take the first right onto May Road, go north about 1 mile and turn right to continue on May Road and then curve left with the road. Turn left onto Sand Bay Road (don't get confused that straight is Sand Bay Point Road), then take the first left on Sand Bay Lane—got it? Sign for the parking area should be on your left with a short walking path to the beach. No fee, should be a port-a-potty.

Directions to Sand Bay 1 Beach:

44.8564, -87.4984. From Highway 57, turn north on Stone Road and go approximately 3 miles, turn left onto Highway County C, then take the first right onto May Road, go north about 1 mile and turn right to continue on May Road and then curve left with the road. Continue straight when May Road turns into Sand Bay Point Road. When Sand Bay Point Road curves to the left, go straight on Sand Bay Lane which leads to the water's edge.

Kayak Wisconsin, Door County Peninsula

The public access is between the trailer park and the resort. No fee, no parking lot, no restrooms.

Directions to Cliff View Drive Beach:

44.8788, -87.4570. From Highway 57/42, turn north on Idlewild Road which turns into Highway County M. It is about 5 miles from Highway 57/42 until you turn left on High Cliff Park Road, then take the first right onto Cliff View Drive, keep straight on Cliff View Drive to the beach on Green Bay. This is a small public access, no fee, no restrooms.

Directions to Sherwood Point Road:

44.8881, -87.4342. For a quieter take out spot, go up to Sherwood Point Road: Off of Highway 57/42 turn north on Idlewild Road which turns into County M after you cross County C. County M curves right up into Sherwood Point, turn right (south) onto Sherwood Point Road (away from the lighthouse) to Sawyer Harbor. It is recommended you stop at the water's edge. . . There is a launch fee but no restrooms.

Bluffs, Beaches, Lighthouses and Shipwrecks

Directions to Potawatomi State Park boat ramp:

44.8781, -87.4268. Boat ramp: From Highway 57 turn north on County PD (Park Drive), then take a right onto Park Entrance Road. To get to the boat launch take a left onto South Norway Road (going north- does that confuse you?) to its end at Shoreline Road–take a left (north again) onto Shoreline Road up to the boat ramp. State park fee, restrooms at the boat launch.

Directions to Sherwood Point Lighthouse:

44.8928, -87.4335. Off of Highway 57/42, turn north on Idlewild Road which turns into County M after you cross County C. County M curves right up into Sherwood Point, turn left (north) onto Sherwood Point Road. Remember, the Lighthouse is a private Coast Guard owned property. Please enjoy the view of the lighthouse from the road.

Kayak Wisconsin, Door County Peninsula

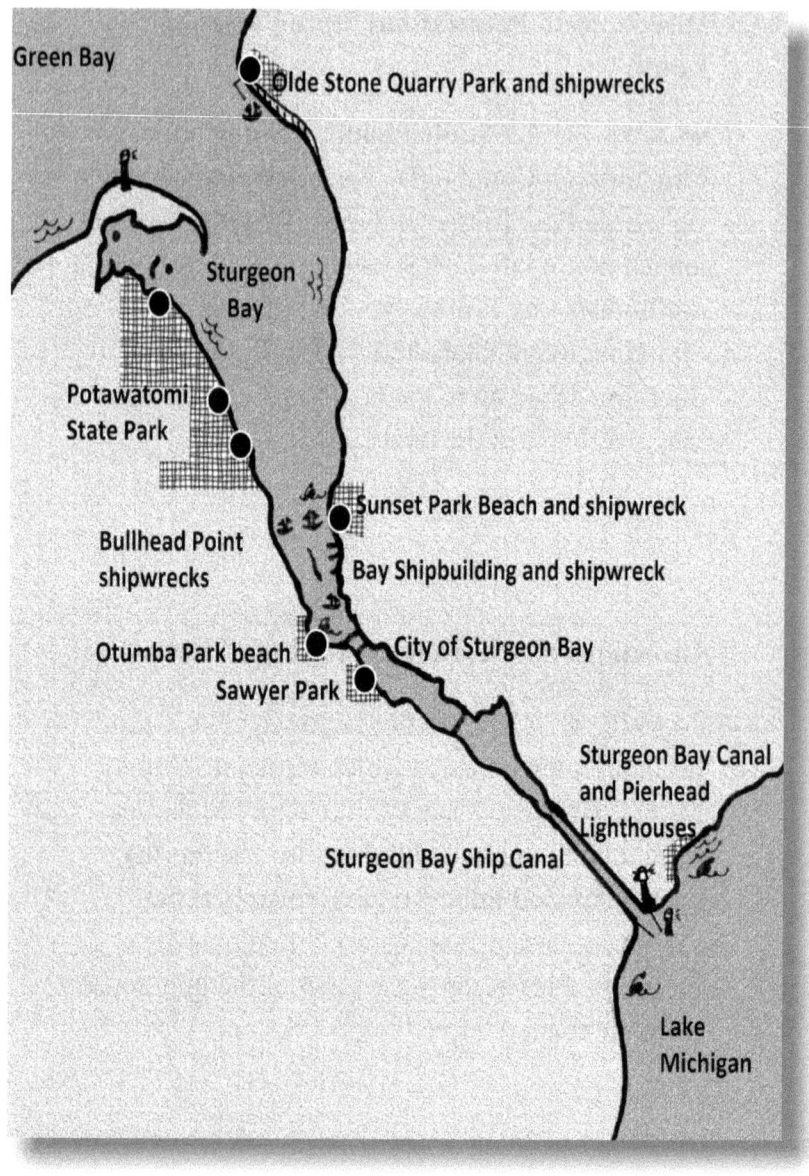

Bluffs, Beaches, Lighthouses and Shipwrecks

Leg 7

Sturgeon Bay

Potawatomi State Park through Sturgeon Bay to Lake Michigan

With Olde Stone Quarry Park, shipbuilding, two great lighthouses and lots of shipwrecks

10 miles

Windy, oh so windy... This paddle took a long time for us to decide. It was our choice in Autumn, when Plan A: kayaking the Green Bay side of Door County was not navigable because of high winds and a small craft advisory. No problem, there is always a quiet "lee" side to Door County. So, we drove to the Lake Michigan side for Plan B and stood looking out from the shore at two foot white caps pounding on the shore, kind of looked like fun, until we noticed our first timer Wayla big eyed— so we chose Plan C: Sturgeon Bay and the Sturgeon Bay channel.

This paddle is a full tour of the largest bay in the Door Peninsula, Sturgeon Bay, down to the city of Sturgeon Bay which is at the natural end of the bay, and then through the Sturgeon Bay shipping canal. You will start in the west end of Sturgeon Bay by Green Bay, and along the way tour Potawatomi State Park, the Olde Stone Quarry,

Kayak Wisconsin, Door County Peninsula

several parks in the city of Sturgeon Bay, see shipbuilding in progress and the opportunity to see lots of shipwrecks (maybe that's why they keep building more) and end at the eastern end of the Sturgeon Bay shipping Canal on Lake Michigan with several famous lighthouses: the Sturgeon Bay Canal Lighthouse and the Pier head Lighthouses.

Our Leg 7 paddle is easily condensed to a variety of shorter paddles. You can put in at Potawatomi State Park, play in Sawyer Harbor and then cross Sturgeon Bay to the beautiful white cliffs of Olde Stone Quarry County Park for a 2 mile crossing. To explore the lower peninsula of Sturgeon Bay, put in at Potawatomi State Park and follow the beautiful shoreline of the park to the city of Sturgeon Bay and the Sturgeon Bay channel and then take out at the Coast Guard Station when you arrive at Lake Michigan for an 8 mile paddle. To cut Sturgeon Bay in half as we did, there are several places in downtown Sturgeon Bay to take out: beautiful Sunset Park, Sawyer Park Boat Landing, or the quieter Otumba Park beach.

Put in at Potawatomi State Park's boat landing in Sawyer Harbor. The park is named in honor of the tribe that inhabited Green Bay's shores and islands when Europeans first settled the area. The tribe called themselves Bo-De-Wad-Me which means "keeper of the sacred fire." Eventually the spelling and pronunciation were changed to Potawatomi. Potawatomi is such a fun name to say and you just want to start drumming as you say it Pot a wat o me, Pot a wat o me.

Potawatomi State Park is a great place for a first timer to learn the fundamentals of kayaking as Sawyer Harbor is protected from the winds off of Green Bay. 'Sure glad we took the time to paddle around the south end of the harbor around the little tiny island. Beautiful swans a swimmin' with two baby "cygnets". We got a little too close for daddy "cob" swan and he started spreading his wings and standing up on the water. Reverse! Reverse! All kayak engines in reverse! Heard a kayak legend that a kayaker actually drowned from a swan attack—they can actually run across the water with a ten foot wingspan to attack to protect their babes, and the kayaker tipped over and couldn't get back up because the swan kept attacking. Let's not find out if that story could be true, so all kayak armies in retreat! Daddy "cob" calmed down, but kept up a sentinel march back and forth to protect his family.

So off we retreated out of Sawyer Harbor. You could paddle along the Potawatomi State Park shoreline along the southern Door Peninsula for more than two miles of a quiet, serene naturally

Kayak Wisconsin, Door County Peninsula

relaxing paddle. Slip up onto the shore at Mary's Waterfront Bar and Grill immediately after the park for a patio lunch and beverage.

We chose to cross the channel to the White Cliffs of Dover–oh wait–wrong cliffs, wrong, channel…the cliffs across Sturgeon Bay are actually the white Olde Stone Quarry dolomite walls. Take the time to notice the beautiful white dolomite cliff walls of the quarry, the wood piling along the shore, and see if you can find the two sunken barges by the fishing pier. Find the two large triangle cement anchors on land then the huge anchor chains still in the water.

After the spectacular view of the Olde Stone Quarry escarpment, paddle down into the largest bay of Door County—Sturgeon Bay. Sturgeon Bay is by far the biggest of the best of the Door Peninsula's bays—7 miles long before they added the channel for another 1.3 miles! Naming the bay "Sturgeon Bay" is so apt because it is named after Wisconsin's biggest fish—the lake sturgeon. Wisconsin's sturgeons are so ancient they have outlived the dinosaurs. The lake sturgeon is distinctive for its long sleek body with no fish scales and can grow up to 12 feet, weigh more than 125 pounds, and live more than 100 years. Dun dun dun, Dun dun dun, oh wait—edit out the Jaws theme song, never heard of the giant sturgeon attacking a kayak. . .but this amazing fish is absolutely worthy of giving its name to Sturgeon Bay.

Sturgeon Bay is a great choice to kayak on a windy day. Wayla, our first timer, asked about the little white frothy top of the waves, she thought they were suspiciously similar to the dangerous "white caps" she had heard about. "Yeah, but they are only little one footers in the calmer Sturgeon Bay. Since the wind is blowing from Green Bay, the waves are actually helping push us along. If you time your paddle strokes just right, you can actually surf the top of the waves. . . just call us Surfin' Dudes"!

Surf down to Sunset Park in Sturgeon Bay (it'll be on your left). It is a big park on 3rd Avenue with a boat/kayak launch, a nice sandy beach, and an inland Little Bradley lake. You could bring some Frisbee golf discs and stop and play the 6 hole course. This park is named for its famous sunsets, so you might be enticed to stay and enjoy it. The poor steam barge Joys built in Milwaukee caught fire in 1898 and now lies broken in about 10 feet of water about 300 feet off shore of the western edge of Sunset Park.

Next to Sunset Park is the Bay Shipbuilding Company. They have been building ships in

Kayak Wisconsin, Door County Peninsula

Sturgeon Bay since 1918 and were quite active in the war effort for the US Army from 1940-1945. Bay Shipbuilding continues to build, see how close you can get to the ships being built. While you are looking up at the huge ships, look down too, the Adriatic, a schooner (and then she was converted to one of the first self-unloaders by the Leatham and Smith Sturgeon Bay Ship Company) was sadly abandoned and sank right underneath the shipbuilding pier. She lies in about 15 feet of water just northwest of the historic Michigan Street Bridge and is now on the National Register of Historic Places.

Across the bay is Bullhead Point, a small public park, famous for great views and folks fishing, so share nicely. Most importantly, there are three, count them THREE shipwrecks here. The Empire State was a wooden passenger steamer, the Ida Corning, was a two masted schooner and the Oak

Leaf was a three masted schooner—both carried lumber. All three were later cut down to barges and sadly abandoned and burned at this pier in 1931. Lucky for us, they are in only about 6 feet of water and easily seen from kayaks, sadly for them, this means that as they pop out above water they will decay much faster.

In the middle of the bay there is a small reef called Dunlap Reef. Depending on water level you will be able to see it, or it may be a few inches below the water, so watch out! This is a historic site as there once was a lighthouse on the reef from 1881 to 1924. The lighthouse was sold and moved to 4th Street in Sturgeon Bay and is now a private residence minus its lantern light room.

On the right, west, mainland side of Sturgeon Bay is Otumba Park. It is a small little park with a wonderful sandy beach and is an official kayak launch site that could be an alternative take out spot or another great spot for a picnic.

Now you are in downtown Sturgeon Bay as you pass under the historic steel Michigan Street Bridge. It is a 1930 bascule drawbridge steel overhead truss type bridge that is the only example of its type in Wisconsin and was perfect for windy Sturgeon Bay. The Michigan Street

Bridge was initially the only bridge across the bay. It is on the National Register of Historic Places and has inspired a Steel Bridge songfest in Sturgeon Bay. At the north side of the Michigan Street Bridge is another unidentified shipwreck with a broken hull mostly buried in 10 feet of water. Perhaps that is why we were unsuccessful in locating it, better luck to you.

Between the two bridges is the Door County Maritime Museum and the big red fireboat which offers cruises. The red Fred A Busse fireboat was built in 1937 and served the city of Chicago for many years.

Glide under new Oregon Street Bridge, built to replace the old historic Michigan Street Bridge. It is a drawbridge that is sure to open for the big kayaks coming through. . .umm, perhaps you shouldn't wait for that.

Right after the Oregon Street Bridge is the Sawyer Park Boat Launch. The park does require a launch fee because it is a big park which has a 6 lane boat ramp, restrooms with showers, fish cleaning stations, picnic area with grills, and a Gazebo. In the Dock master's building there is a special TV that provides up-to-the-minute weather maps and conditions, very helpful on such a windy fall day!

Bluffs, Beaches, Lighthouses and Shipwrecks

The Sawyer Park boat landing is where we took out in Autumn, because we have a family tradition of doing the Schopf's Dairy View Corn Maze on County Highway I just south of Egg Harbor. We divide into two teams and race through the corn maze—still takes an hour or two. Not that we are competitive or anything, but we are known to hunch down and whisper so the other team doesn't know where we are. This corn maze is the BEST we've ever seen anywhere and you must use the map to guide you, or there is sincere doubt you would ever find your way out. Another great way to end an Autumn day in Wisconsin in Door County.

Sunshine on my shoulders makes me happy as we start the second half of our Sturgeon Bay paddle in downtown Sturgeon Bay. Just up on Madison Street, Bay Shore Outfitters offers kayak rentals and sales along with stand up paddleboards (SUP's) and accessories. So bring a friend and rent another kayak! Bay Shore Outfitters is also a great resource for information for kayaking the Door Peninsula.

We launched on an incredible calm, warm summer day at Otumba Park beach—a very peaceful entry spot and gave us the chance to see the historic Michigan Street Bridge once again.

After the two downtown bridges comes the extremely tall Bayview Bridge. It is as much fun to float under the bridge and look up as it is to walk across the bridge and look down. The "bypass" or highway bridge was built in 1978 and was a real relief from the traffic jams that used to clog the Michigan Street Bridge especially during the summer months. Although it is 228 feet long and really high, it isn't always lofty enough, so it is also a drawbridge that opens for those even taller ships or sailboats.

Pleasantly paddle past yachts and sailboats, it is leisurely fun to explore Sturgeon Bay's waterfront. The city of Sturgeon Bay is located at the natural end of Sturgeon Bay, before they cut it in half to create the Sturgeon Bay channel. OK, the channel was fairly needed since it is a longggg way to go around the entire Door Peninsula and somewhat of a danger—based on the many shipwreck locations there are. So in 1870 the canal was started but did not open for large ships until 1890.

Cruising through the one and a third mile Sturgeon Bay ship canal is not for the faint of heart. The charter fishing excursion boats head

Bluffs, Beaches, Lighthouses and Shipwrecks

down the channel along with all the other yachts and boats creating a parade of boats. Most making big wakes that challenge paddling in the narrow channel, especially as not only is there the wakes to attend to, but the waves bounce off the channel wall and attack again.

The reward comes as you approach Lake Michigan and on the left port side of the boat you will glimpse the Sturgeon Bay Ship Canal Lighthouse. This is another historical lighthouse built in 1898 with its circular lantern room with custom curved glass and diamond astragals on the windows and has a third order freznel lens. The lighthouse is quite striking with its white coat of

paint against the brilliant blue sky. Initially it was painted brown which made it hard to see, but they quickly saw the error of their ways and switched it to its pretty white coat and red roof.

We rounded the corner north as we came out of the channel inside the pier head walls and landed at the coast guard station. This is a large station built in 1886 for law enforcement on the water and appreciated for their great search and rescue notoriety. Use marine radio channel 22A for information, and for international distress calling (hope you never need it) use marine radio channel 16. The coast guard station beach is sandy and quiet but does not have any public restroom. Considered going behind a bush…but beware this is also a National Homeland Security Station and just may be closely monitored by cameras—chose to hold it. Although there are many signs saying "private property, no access", the beach is a designated kayak launch site and you are OK to use the parking lot and carry in/out your kayak.

After kayaking, change gears, stretch your legs and stroll down the pier (yup, it's public) and get a great closer look at the vivid red Sturgeon Bay pier head lighthouse. It is even older than the channel lighthouse as it was built in 1872. Interestingly, this lighthouse was initially white and later changed to its bright red color.

Kayak Wisconsin, Door County Peninsula

Logistics:

Directions to Potawatomi State Park:

44.8781, -87.4268. Boat ramp: From Highway 57 turn north on County PD (Park Drive), then take a right onto Park Entrance Road. To get to the boat launch take a left onto South Norway Road (going west–does that confuse you?) to its end at Shoreline Road–take a left (west again) onto Shoreline Road up to the boat ramp. There is a great canoe/kayak ramp next to a small dock located to the right of the boat ramps.

44.8635, -87.4108 or 44.8562, -87.4039. Kayak launches: From Highway 57 turn north on County PD (Park Drive), then take a right onto Park Entrance Road. Take a right (east) on South Norway Road to Shoreline Road and take a left onto Shoreline Road. You can park in the parking lot for Hemlock Trailhead and carry your kayak to the water's edge just before the accessible fishing pier, or continue to the small parking lot before Norway Road intersection and again carry your kayak to the water's edge. Our opinion is that the kayak ramp at the boat ramp above is much easier to use.

Bluffs, Beaches, Lighthouses and Shipwrecks

Directions to George Pinney Olde Stone Quarry County Park:

44.9046, -87.4052. Take Walker Road east off of Highway 42 for 2.2 miles, turn left on County HH (Dunn Road) for just .8 miles, then right on Bay Shore Drive (County B) for 1.5 miles to Olde Stone Quarry Park at 4879 Bay Shore Drive.

Directions to Sunset Park in Sturgeon Bay:

44.8449, -87.3860. Take Egg Harbor Road off Highway 57/42 into Sturgeon Bay, take a slight left onto N. 8th Ave (County Road HH), right onto N. 3rd Ave (County Road B), third left onto Sunset Drive into the Park.

Directions to Otumba Park in Sturgeon Bay:

44.8309, -87.3897. Turn north on S. Neenah Street in Sturgeon Bay off of Highway 57/42. Then turn left on E. Maple Street, right on N. Joliet Ave and then the second right onto W. Juniper St to Otumba Park.

Kayak Wisconsin, Door County Peninsula

Directions to Sawyer Park Boat Launch:

44.8283, -87.3799. Take S. Neenah Ave off Highway 57/42 in Sturgeon Bay. Sawyer Park is at the intersection of Neenah Ave and E. Oak St.

Directions to Coast Guard Station, and the Channel and Pierhead Lighthouses:

44.7944, -87.3127. 2501 Canal Road. Cross Sturgeon Bay on the Bayview (Highway 42/57) Bridge and immediately turn right (east) onto Utah St, then turn right at the second intersection on Cove Road, take the first left onto Canal Road (Highway TT) and follow it to the Coast Guard Station and the parking lot. Carry your boat to the beach inside the pier head. You may walk out onto the pier, but please enjoy the Channel lighthouse from the parking area.

Directions to Schopf's Dairy View Corn Maze:

5169 County I, Sturgeon Bay. Take County I east from Highway 42 at Carlsville about 8 miles north of Sturgeon Bay. Schopf's DairyView Farm with is approximately 1 mile west of Hwy 42 on County I. Enjoy the farm tour and corn maze!

Bluffs, Beaches, Lighthouses and Shipwrecks

Shipwreck locations:

Joseph L. Hurd: 44.9037, -87.4055. Lies at the eastern shore of the marina entrance in 15 feet of water at Olde Stone Quarry.

The Mueller: 44.9022, -87.4019. Lies more east after the quarry dock ruins in 10 feet of water at Olde Stone Quarry.

Joys: 44.8488, -87.3890. About 300 feet off shore of the western edge of Sunset Park. Sunset Park is on the north side of Sturgeon Bay off North 3rd Avenue.

Adriatic: 44.8366, -87.3834. Lies in 15 feet of water at the Sturgeon Bay Shipbuilding Company dock, just northwest of the historic Michigan St. Bridge.

Empire State, Ida Corning and the Oak Leaf: 44.8415, -87.3955. Off eastern side of Bullhead Point. Bullhead Point is on the south side of Sturgeon Bay off North Duluth Ave.

Dan Hayes: lies somewhere in Sturgeon Bay in just 15 feet of water, but we were unable to locate it.

Kayak Wisconsin, Door County Peninsula

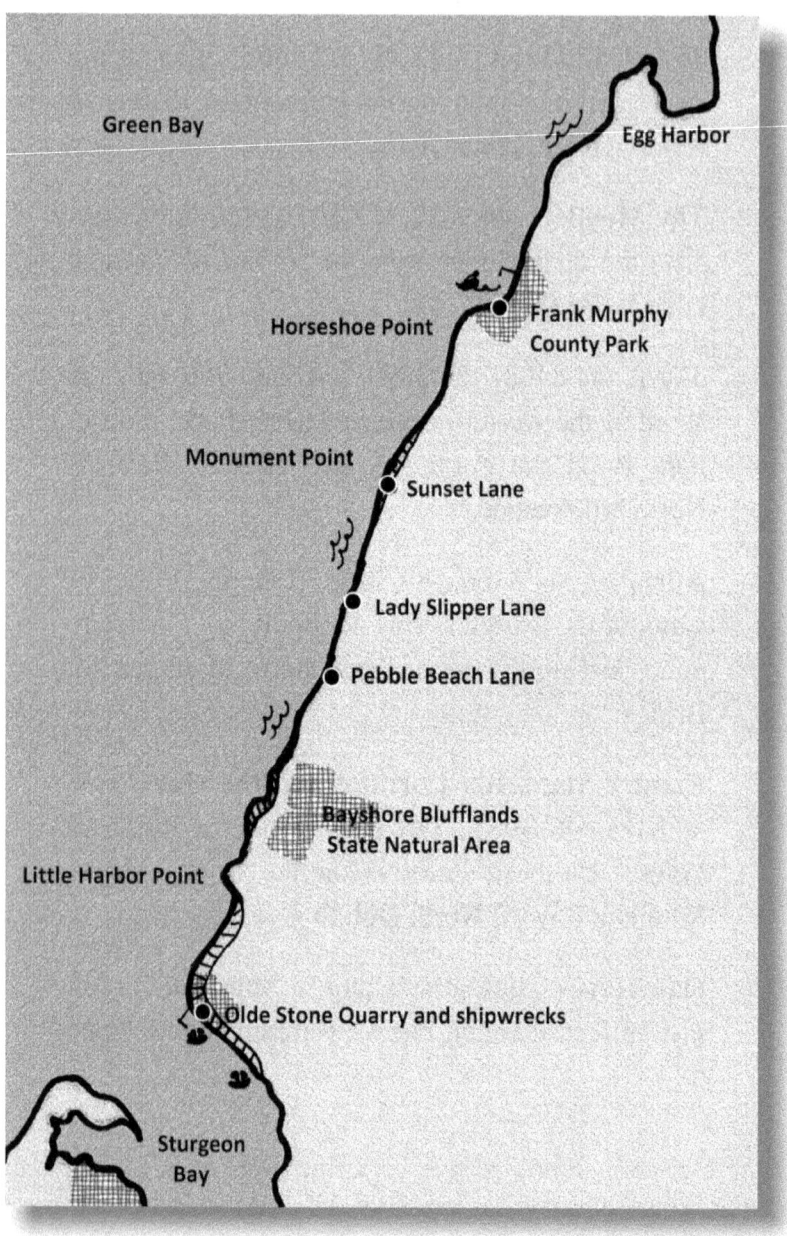

Leg 8

Olde Stone Quarry

Olde Stone Quarry County Park to Frank Murphy County Park
With Pebble Beach, Lady Slipper, and Sunset Lanes
9 miles

The oldies but goodies, Olde Stone Quarry is the fascinating start to this paddle with its sunken ships and shipbuilding anchor and cable, but it doesn't end there. You can explore the pebble beach and look up to the bluffs of the Niagara Escarpment, marvel at the tiny wildflower Lady Slipper orchids, and sunbath at the big sandy beach when you arrive at Frank Murphy County Park. And there is always the added excitement of rumors of Al Capone's hideouts.

There are several ways to shorten this paddle. Lady Slipper Lane off of Bay Shore Drive does run down to the water's edge and is a designated kayak launch area at about a little more than the midway point at 5 miles from Olde Stone Quarry boat landing, and then Lady Slipper Lane to Frank Murphy County Park is 4 miles. Pebble Beach Lane is a little before the midway point and Sunset Lane is after the midway point closer to

Kayak Wisconsin, Door County Peninsula

Frank Murphy County Park–both are also off of Bay Shore Drive (County B).

We put in at the western shore of Door County finally on the peninsula, well really the island, at the historic Olde Stone Quarry, George Pinney County Park. The quarry was in production from 1893 to 1944 producing large stone for harbors around Lake Michigan and crushed stone for roads. The crushed stone was loaded onto ships right at the site. The steel frontage and wooden pilings along the shore are remnants of the quarry dock.

As you paddle out of the marina look for the Joseph L Hurd shipwreck, a wooden steamer built in 1869 and abandoned in 1913 lying on the lake floor at the eastern side of the harbor entrance in about 15 feet of water but stretching to just about the boulder shoreline. Another ship, the Mueller built in 1887 in Manitowoc as a steam barge lies more eastern into Sturgeon Bay at the shoreline after the quarry building ruins, but her steam post, shaft and propeller are on shore by the boat launch. Also try to find the submerged cable from the Peterson Brothers Shipbuilding Company which has two large triangular cement ground anchors on wooden pilings on the shoreline (still there!) which stretched the cable ¼ mile into the

Bluffs, Beaches, Lighthouses and Shipwrecks

bay to attach ships to, to test engines at full throttle.

The Olde Stone Quarry now has a beautiful protected harbor, pavilion, picnic area and restrooms–which are always helpful before hopping into the kayak. The protective harbor was very helpful in giving Justin's brother who is even newer than new to the sport of kayaking a chance to learn the basics and safety recommendations. Rick and Chris's son Rich also joined us for this day.

We made a pal of a seagull at Olde Stone Quarry. OK, OK, technically there is no such thing as a seagull, there are just different varieties of gulls,

and anyway around here we ought to call them "lake" gulls. You are most likely to make friends with a big chested Herring Gull with a white head, yellow bill with red spots, black wing tips and pink legs. They live in Door County all year and love to steal your snack the minute you turn your head. If your buddy is medium sized and his yellow bill has a black ring and his legs are yellow, say hello to mister Ring-Billed Gull. If your new found companion is small with a black head and his wing has a white triangle and he has orange legs, you have made the acquaintance of the less common Bonaparte's Gull, named after Napoleon's nephew. Don't worry because Bonaparte won't steal your dinner, he eats insects and fish. But if you have discovered a huge gull with pink legs and only one red spot on his yellow bill, eureka! You have found a rare Great Black Backed Gull. Now hopefully, you'll find the Door Peninsula most abundant bird much more interesting...

We headed up the coast and really feel like we are in "real" Door County paddling through the Little Harbor (it really is little) towards Little Harbor Point (which they also got right). The shoreline is fairly straight here for most of the paddle, but there are nice rocky cliffs interspersed throughout the area. No actual parks to stop at, but the homes are often tucked away above the cliffs and blend in very nicely. Enjoy the gulls, geese and other wildlife along the water's edge.

An old abandoned resort, Chateau Hutter, caught our eye. The large rustic stone lodge of Chateau Hutter has a wonderful natural limestone patio. There are several stone villas and a cool weathered wood barn right at the water's edge. It's fun to imagine who has all stayed at the resort in its prime—maybe Al Capone? Don't laugh, that is the rumor we heard from another visitor, and there are too many rumors that Al came up from Chicago to hide in Door County to just shoo the notion away. Don't all Illinois folks "Escape to Wisconsin" as an old tourism slogan goes?

Just across Bayshore Drive is the Bay Shore Bluffland Preserve with hiking trails up the 175 foot Niagara Escarpment Bluff to great views of

Kayak Wisconsin, Door County Peninsula

Green Bay, worth a stop all on its own. The property is our first easily accessible Door County Land Trust Preserve. The Door County Land Trust is a great non-governmental, non-profit organization whose mission is to preserve forests, wetlands, and shorelines to help us all enjoy Door County's scenic beauty forever. On our tour around the Door Peninsula we will discover many more Door County Land Trusts acres of public land for us to explore.

Just a mile after Chateau Hutter, take a short break at Pebble's Beach Lane and look for some pretty pebbles to keep for a souvenir. The rounded stones were formed by glaciers thousands of years ago along with the lapping of the waves on the shoreline. It was a gorgeous summer day with hardly a cloud in the sky, so we took this great occasion to wade in over the rocks and enjoy a refreshing swim in the clear waters of Green Bay.

Less than a mile up is Lady Slipper Lane where you can stop and search for Lady Slipper flowers, a type of Wisconsin orchid. They are called Lady Slippers because they tend to have small petals at the top with a bulging flower at the bottom that looks like a petite lady's slipper! You may find Large Yellow Lady Slippers, which really are not large–just larger than the rarer small yellow lady slipper. The Large Yellow Lady Slipper is the most abundant of the orchids in Wisconsin and is the official Door County wildflower and loves the limestone dolomite bluffs and gravel. There are also pink or white lady slippers (becoming rare in Door County because the deer love them–naughty deer) or even Ram's-head lady slipper which looks like a little rams head but are often overlooked because they are so small. Not to be out done, Door County also has the Hookers Orchid which has yellowish green flowers. Wow, take notice and pleasure in the tiny flowers growing in the rock cracks and crannies along the Door Peninsula shoreline.

A little more than a mile up the coast is Sunset Lane. The western shoreline of the Door Peninsula is the eastern side of Green Bay and is famous for fantastic sunsets. We were too early, but stay or come back to this spot for a spectacular view as the sun slowly sets in the west. . .

After a bit of merlot, we continued on our paddle all the way past Monument Shoal to Monument Point. Monument Point barely bumps out into the bay. Monument bluff does have some rocky cliffs, still hard to imagine why they chose to call it Monument Point. Paddle a little further to Horseshoe Point which kick butts Monument Point in size.

Kayak Wisconsin, Door County Peninsula

Round the corner of Horseshoe Point and travel into what else—Horseshoe Bay, which is a gently quiet bay actually in the shape of a horseshoe as most bays probably are. Frank Murphy County Park is in the bay and is quite easy to locate. The boat launch is at the southern end and a bit away from the huge brown dock.

Seems we chose the day for the annual triathlon at the park, but all the commotion was over by the time we arrived. Check to be sure you don't pick the busiest day of the year to paddle into the park.

Generally speaking, Murphy Park is a pleasant park with a wonderful public sandy beach, pavilion, playground area, and woods to explore. There is a volleyball court if you want some more exercise after your paddle. And of course, the appreciated restrooms after a fun day on the water and keeping hydrated with lots of water.

Are you ready for some more mystery? There is a hidden tunnel at Frank Murphy County Park that supposedly extends three miles to Egg Harbor. Rumors fly that this was a tunnel used by Al Capone as a quick get-away from the "feds" when they searched for him at the pub in Egg Harbor. Another story is that the tunnel is actually a natural cave that Chief Tecumseh, of the Ottawa

Tribe, used for escaping from other tribes. Exciting history abounds in Door County.

Logistics:

Directions to Olde Stone Quarry George Pinney County Park:

44.9046, -87.4052. Take Walker Road west off of Highway 42 just north of Sturgeon Bay for 2.2 miles, turn left on County HH (Dunn Road) for just .8 miles, then right on Bay Shore Drive (County B) for 1.5 miles to Olde Stone Quarry Park at 4879 Bay Shore Drive. Fee to launch, restrooms available.

Directions to Pebble Beach Lane public access:

44.9558, -87.3756. From highway 42 turn west on Carlsville Road, when it ends at Bay Shore Drive (County B) turn right/north. After Cedar Road, turn left on Pebble Beach Lane to the bay. No fee, but no restrooms or parking lot.

Kayak Wisconsin, Door County Peninsula

Directions to Lady Slipper Lane public access:

44.9653, -87.3708. From Highway 42 turn west on Carlsville Road, when it ends at Bay Shore Drive (County B) turn right/north, at the second Lady Slipper Lane turn left to the bay. No fee, no restrooms, park on the dead end road.

Directions to Sunset Lane public access:

44. 9839, -87.3621. From Highway 42 go west on Monument Point Road to Bay Shore Drive. Turn left/south on Bay Shore Drive to the first right- Sunset Lane to the bay. No fee, no restrooms, park on dead end road.

Directions to Frank Murphy County Park:

45.0138, -87.3341. From Highway 42 go north on County G. At the T intersection go left on Horseshoe Bay Road. Frank Murphy County Park is at the intersection of Horseshoe Bay Road and Bay Shore Drive in the town of Egg Harbor. Fee to launch, but there is a parking lot and restrooms.

Bluffs, Beaches, Lighthouses and Shipwrecks

Shipwreck location:

Joseph L. Hurd: 44.9037, -87.4055. Lies at the eastern shore of the marina entrance in 15 feet of water at Olde Stone Quarry.

The Mueller: 44.9022, -87.4019. Lies more east after the quarry dock ruins in on the shore and into 10 feet of water at Olde Stone Quarry.

Directions to Bayshore Blufflands State Natural Area:

Lower trailhead: 44.9349, -87.3907. 5457 Bayshore Drive. From Highway 42 north of Sturgeon Bay, turn west on Carlsville Road and drive for 2.2 miles, then turn left on Bayshore Drive. The parking area for the trailhead will be .9 miles.

Upper trailhead: 44.9379, -87.3680. 5517 Reynolds Road. From Highway 42 north of Sturgeon Bay, turn west on Town Line Road and drive 1.5 miles, then turn right/north on Reynolds Road for .5 miles to the parking area.

Kayak Wisconsin, Door County Peninsula

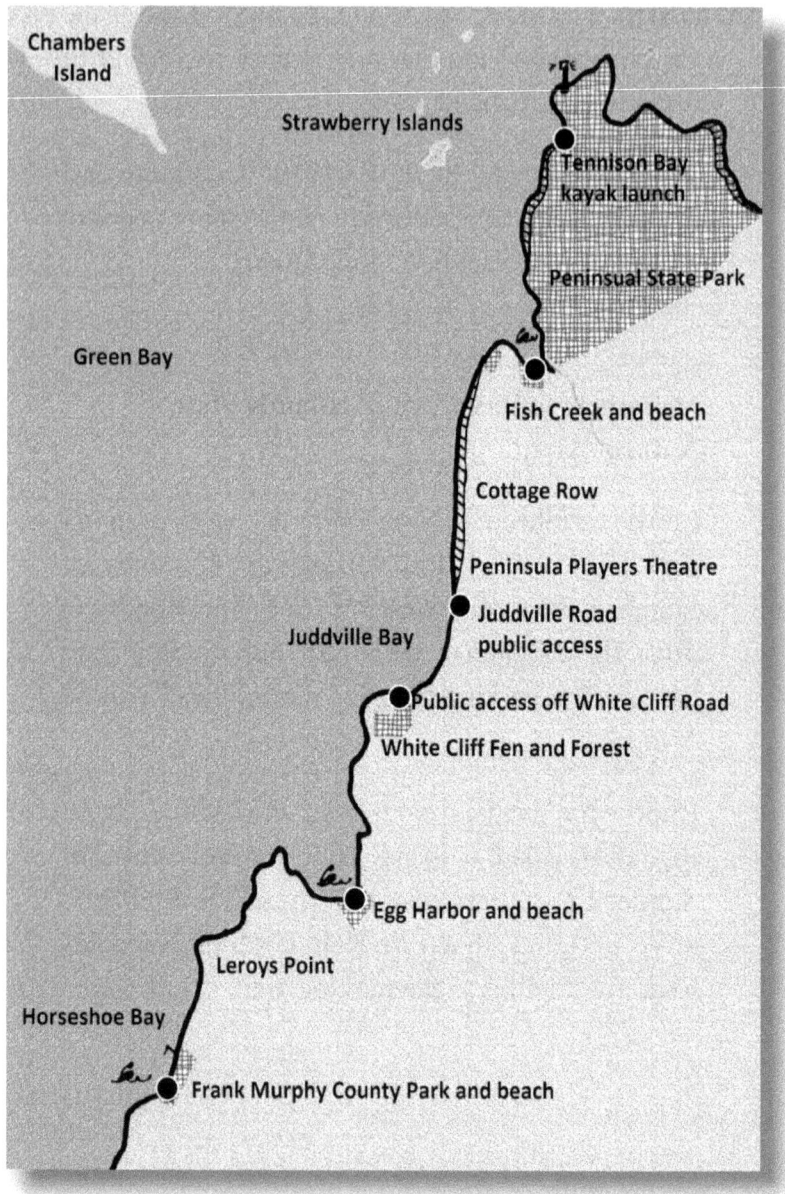

Leg 9

Tour of the Towns

Frank Murphy County Park to Peninsula State Park
With Egg Harbor, Fish Creek:
the towns, the beaches, the sunsets
11.5 miles

Sunset Boulevard–no,no, this is much better! Sunsets with red, pink, blue, purple and more as the sun begins to set over Green Bay. Lots of highlights in this tour, not just of two of Door County's finest towns; Egg Harbor and Fish Creek, but also beautiful beaches for swimming, the best island views of all Door County; Chamber Island and the four little Strawberry Islands, and ending at the largest Door County State Park, Peninsula State Park. Oh, and don't forget to stay for the awesome sunsets!

This, a little longer than 10 miles day paddle, can be cut in half or thirds to give time to explore the Door County towns of Egg Harbor–which has a brew pub and has one of our favorite shops, and Fish Creek–the best strolling and shopping district in Door County! It would be about 3 ½ miles to Egg Harbor, 6 miles to Fish Creek and then 2 ½ miles to Tennison Bay in Peninsula State Park.

Kayak Wisconsin, Door County Peninsula

However, we like our kayaking the nature way, starting at Frank Murphy County Park, stretching half way at peaceful Juddville Road public access and then ending at beautiful Tennison Bay kayak launch at Peninsula State Park.

We docked our "chase car" at Tennison Bay's boat landing in Peninsula State Park for our take out point, and slipped into the bay at Frank Murphy County Park on a quiet day. Murphy County Park has the best sandy beach of this whole paddle, so if you would like to swim–jump in now. The beach is a favorite sunbather spot and many boats anchor here for the great sand and camaraderie. We paddled across Horseshoe Bay which does sort of look like a horseshoe, or perhaps, there is actually a horseshoe lost in the bay and you could try to find it. . .

The first point is Leroy's Point–not sure what made Leroy so famous, but since it is just a little point guess he only had his 15 minutes of fame–just enough to get a point named after him. Paddle 'round the next big point into Egg Harbor. The town of Egg Harbor is in the bay itself. The sunsets around this area are spectacular!

In the bay at Egg Harbor, the town has a big marina with a public boat landing that is a possible put in/take out spot, but the public beach next to it is the easiest place for a kayak launch or just to stop and have a picnic, or in our case a famous Wisconsin fish fry as Rick fried up some pan fish, the bay does have great perch. Or you could go into town and sample another Door County favorite, the "must do" fish boil. The Fish Boil is a Scandinavian tradition with boiling white fish in a cast iron kettle over a blazing bonfire which ends in the famous dramatic fiery shooting flames where the water boils over and the fish is perfectly cooked. The Fish Boil experience is as fun to watch as it is to eat!

In Egg Harbor, you could check out a Door County microbrewery, the Shipwrecked Brew Pub. Wisconsin is famous for its beer and you can't get more Wisconsinish than a mug of local beer and a plate of fish. The Shipwrecked Brew Pub is supposedly haunted by Al Capone's son. There are in fact, tunnels under the building and Egg Harbor that run as far as Frank Murphy County Park–where Al Capone allegedly used as a "get away" spot! Makes you want to turn around and recheck out the park to see if you can find the tunnel doesn't it?

Egg Harbor may have gotten its name from settlers who gathered duck and seagull eggs on the shore, or a more legendary tale is the seagull "egg battle" that took place when the first settlers fought literally with eggs to be the first to land in the harbor in 1825. We didn't find any nests with eggs, but did enjoy watching all the sailboats in and around Egg Harbor. Door County, besides being a burgeoning kayaking haven, is also known as a great destination for yachting and sailing.

After Egg Harbor, the white cliff's of the White Cliff Fen and Forest State Natural Area begin, but from the water all you can see is green cliffs so perhaps the name should be changed. . . This area is the Niagara Escarpment coming all the way from Niagara Falls. The White Cliff Fen and Forest trailhead parking is at the shoreline public access off of White Cliff Road. The forest is undisturbed acres of old growth white cedar, birch, hemlock, oak, maple and aspen. At the base of the Niagara Escarpment is the fen, a

Bluffs, Beaches, Lighthouses and Shipwrecks

marshy area where you will find marsh fern, marsh marigold, marsh milkweed and then bog goldenrod and bog aster. Might want to bring your boots. . .

Just north of the White Cliff Natural area, is Juddville Bay with peaceful Juddville Road just about in the middle. Sounds pretty countrified, but this is about half way in our paddle and is a good quiet spot for a lunch, sunset, or use this as your take out spot to make this an approximate 5-6 mile day paddle depending on how close you stay to the shoreline.

Not feeling quite ready to kayak on your own? Don't own a kayak? Have no fear, Door County Kayak Tours is located inland from Juddville Road on Highway 42. They offer tours to the caves, bluffs, lighthouses and shipwrecks. They offer tours in the morning, afternoon, sunset, and peaceful moonlight tours. Sometimes a little lesson from a pro might come in handy.

Just shortly after Juddville Road is the home of America's oldest summer theater, Peninsula Players, with its theatre in a garden on the shores of Green Bay. Peninsula Players have been offering summer theatre since 1935. The theatre pavilion is open on the sides to expand the tranquil atmosphere and beauty of the gardens.

Kayak Wisconsin, Door County Peninsula

There is a nightly bonfire in the beer garden along the shore. Put your paddle in deeper. . .we have a sunset play to catch!

As you paddle north you go past Cottage Row—they actually call it that, although what constitutes a "cottage" in Door County would be a beautiful home to most of us. This area is quite pretty with large boulder bluffs with incredible homes to gawk at. As you kayak toward the curve of the Fish Creek point, there is a small park called Sunset Beach which is the at the end of Main Street in the town of Fish Creek, as the name of the park indicates, it is a favorite local view point for sunsets.

Round the point and paddle into the town of Fish Creek. Fish Creek was the first town to have a pier to provide lumber to passing ships for steam engines. If you go into the marina area, there is a public boat dock along with grassy Clark Park where there are restrooms available. As you paddle out of the marina, between docks is the Fish Creek sand beach and it is permissible to take out or launch kayaks at the beach. There is actually a creek at the end of the bay that gives its name to the town. This creek helps drain the western edge of the Niagara Escarpment.

Bluffs, Beaches, Lighthouses and Shipwrecks

Past the creek at the north end of the bay in shallow three feet of water, lies an unidentified shipwreck of a wooden scow, easy area to explore.

Fish Creek is a good stopping spot to walk about and shop all the famed boutiques. Door County is renowned for its eclectic unique artisan boutiques with paintings, pottery, jewelry and more. Whatever sparks your imagination and passion you will find along Fish Creek's tree lined village streets with their renovated historic buildings housing the galleries and boutiques. Leave space in your kayak hatches for all your finds!

The Fish Creek area gives you the best views towards the large Chambers Island, the biggest island in Green Bay with a decommissioned lighthouse and a newer steel tower lighthouse that can be seen from 10 miles away and certainly from Fish Creek, and the four little Strawberry Islands: Adventure, Little Strawberry, Jack, and tiny Pirate Island–pretty on the horizon and used to be known for strawberry patches–but all are now privately owned.

At Fish Creek, Peninsula State Park begins, which is the largest and most popular of the Door County State Parks and of all Wisconsin with its seven miles of shoreline. As you leave Fish Creek

Kayak Wisconsin, Door County Peninsula

and start paddling past Peninsula State Park, there is a simple kayak launch site off Shore Road. The little point in the bay is Weborg Point, with a concrete pier at the tip. Weborg Point is popular with folks at the park for its great bay view, especially at sunset and is a designated kayak launch site. If you paddle past the point in May, look for warblers at this is a major migration stopover for them. The next little point is Nelson Point. Continue past the shoreline where the Sunset hiking trail (sunsets are beginning to be a common theme aren't they?) follows the shore, so wave at the hikers and bicyclists as you go past.

Peninsula State Park is home to the Northern Sky Theater with its little corner theater in the woods

under the nightly stars. Here, the theater is close enough you can touch it!

We travel into Tennison Bay to the kayak boat ramp. This is a nice shallow bay so there is little large boat traffic and a great take out spot. The ramp is on the south side of the bay as you round into the bay. Time your paddle well and stay for the sunset!

Logistics:

Directions to Frank Murphy County Park

45.0143, -87.3313. From Highway 42 go north on County G. At the T intersection go left on Horseshoe Bay Road. Frank Murphy County Park is at the intersection of Horseshoe Bay Road and Bay Shore Drive in the town of Egg Harbor.

Directions to Egg Harbor Beach Park

45.0456, -87.2859. 4736 Beach Road. Take State Hwy. 42 to Hwy. G. Turn west at the first stop sign down the hill to the parking area.

Kayak Wisconsin, Door County Peninsula

Directions to White Cliff Road public access:

45.0776, -87.2718. From Highway 42 in Egg Harbor, turn west onto White Cliff Road and follow the road as it curves north for 3.1 miles and turn left on public access road. There is a small parking area by the shoreline. This is also the parking for the trailhead for White Cliff Fen and Forest State Natural Area.

Directions to Juddville Road public access:

45.0863, -87.2627. From highway 42, go west on Juddville Road towards the bay. Take a right at the fork in the road and follow the road to the end at the bay.

Directions to Fish Creek Beach:

45.1275, -87.2431. The public beach is directly off of Highway 42 (Main Street) in downtown Fish Creek.

Directions to Peninsula State Park kayak launch off Shore Road:

Bluffs, Beaches, Lighthouses and Shipwrecks

45.1289, -87.2390. Enter the park off of Highway 42 at State Park Road by Fish Creek which turns into Shore Road. Immediately after the park headquarters turn left into the parking area. Long carry in access especially with low lake levels.

Directions to Weborg Point kayak launch at Peninsula State Park:

45.1339, -87.2404. Enter the park off of Highway 42 at State Park Road by Fish Creek which turns into Shore Road. Follow Shore Road for less than 1 mile to Weborg Point parking area. Shower and restrooms available.

Directions to Tennison Bay Canoe/Kayak launch at Peninsula State Park:

45.1619, -87.2350. Enter the park off of Highway 42 at State Park Road which turns into Shore Road. Take a left and continue on Shore Road where it meets with Bluff Road. The kayak launch ramp is in the Tennison Bay Campground– turn left to the ramp by the shore.

Kayak Wisconsin, Door County Peninsula

Shipwreck location:

Unidentified wreck: 45.1315, -87.2391. Northeast side of Fish Creek Harbor after the boat dock, beach and creek.

Peninsula Players Theatre in a garden:

45.0906,-87.2608. Peninsula Players Road, Fish Creek. From Highway 42 between Egg Harbor and Fish Creek, turn west on Peninsula Players Road and follow it about ½ mile to the theatre.

Northern Sky Theater:

45.1645, -87.2258. 10169 Shore Road, Peninsula State Park. From Highway 42 south of Ephraim, turn west on Shore Road into Peninsula State Park. Drive for 3 miles, parking area is on your left.

Kayak Wisconsin, Door County Peninsula

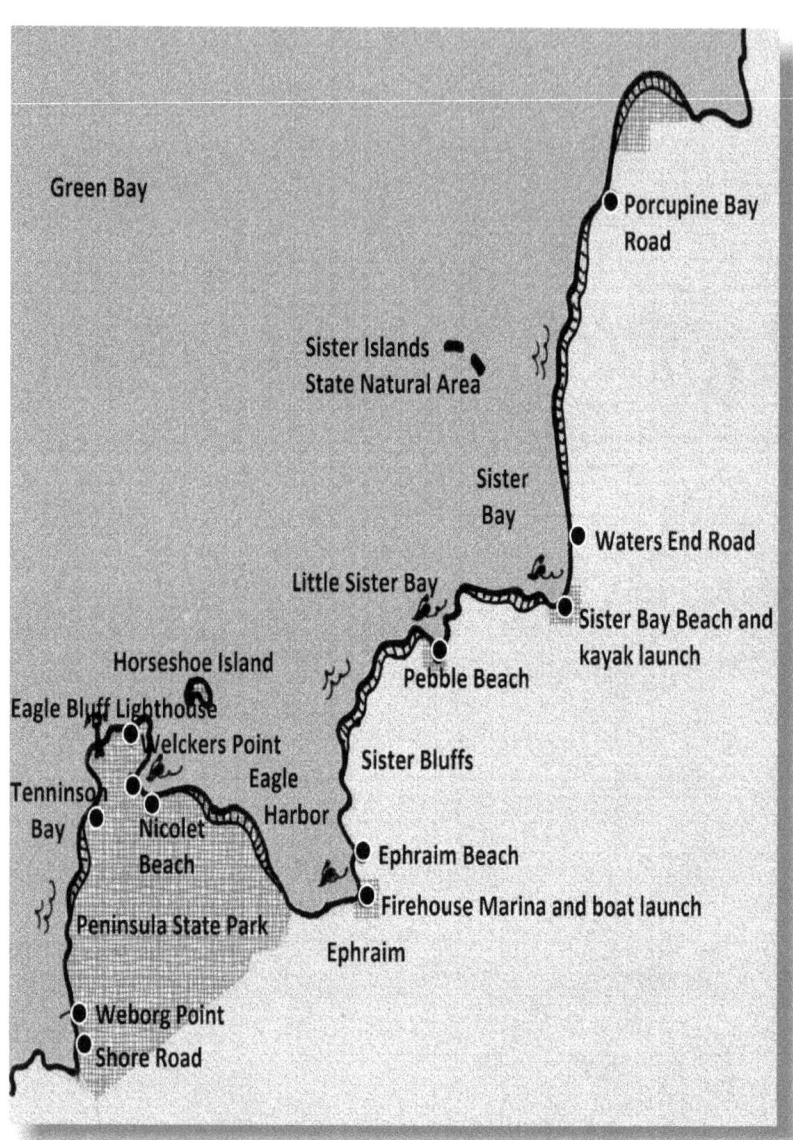

Leg 10

Sister Islands

Peninsula State Park to Porcupine Bay Road
With Sister Islands, OR
Ephraim and Sister Bay and Bluffs
10 miles

Sister Rivalry, which is our favorite: Sister Islands, Sister Bluffs, Little Sister and Sister Bay, or the town of Sister Bay? It is such a difficult choice. Along the way is Peninsula State Park's Eagle Bluff Lighthouse, the beach, the bluffs, Horseshoe Island, Ephraim with its unique Norwegian heritage, and even a shipwreck to look for!

We chose to head out to open seas and see the Sister Islands, but if you do not like being one or more miles off shore, then you may want to hug the shoreline and explore the towns of Ephraim and Sister Bay and follow the majestic bluffs that are a highlight on this paddle. From the Tennison Bay kayak launch in Peninsula State Park to Ephraim it is about 4 miles, then from Ephraim out of Eagle Harbor and around the point into Sister Bay it is another 4 miles, and lastly from the town of Sister Bay to Porcupine Bay Road

Kayak Wisconsin, Door County Peninsula

public access—our planned take out location it is about 6 miles.

Oh what a beautiful morning, oh what a beautiful day. . . We launched at the beautiful Tennison Bay canoe/kayak launch in Peninsula State Park again, it is very shallow and doesn't allow big boats in the bay so it is very serene with great greenery all around. There are however quite a plethora of choices for kayak launching in the large Peninsula State Park including along Shore Road, Weborg Point, Welckers Point on the shore of Green Bay, Nicolet Bay boat landing, and Nicolet Bay beach which also offers kayak rentals, so bring some folks along.

From Tennison Bay, head north around the bluff on the point and quickly the Eagle Bluff Lighthouse comes into view. The three story, cream colored brick lighthouse is perched on top of a 76 foot high cliff walls topped with a 10 sided lantern room with a 3 ½ order frenzel lens that shines 16 miles on a clear night to help ships pass through Strawberry channel created by the Strawberry Islands lying just off your port or left side in the bay of Green Bay. The lighthouse has been fully restored as a tribute to all the light keepers who kept our ancestors safe on dark and stormy nights. It even has some of the original furnishings which you can see if you tour the lighthouse.

Travel along Welckers Point and either head into Nicolet Bay which has a nice public swimming beach or head out towards Horseshoe Island, which is part of the state park and is named for its shape with a dock and boat landing in its harbor. We just had to stop on Horseshoe Island because the explorer Jean Nicolet once landed here. The island has a hiking trail around the perimeter of the 38 acre island for great views of the Strawberry Islands and Ephraim. If you are ready for a bathroom break, it has a pit toilet too.

Travel along the Nicolet Bay bluffs into historic Ephraim which prides itself on its Moravian and Norwegian heritage with century old buildings. Even the public beach has been there since 1934. Ephraim is the home of the red and white Wilson's restaurant that serves humongous sundaes, big enough for the whole family–you gotta stop and have one at least once, it's a Door County tradition! Ephraim does have a boat landing at the Firehouse Marina that can be used for a kayak launch–but the designated kayak launch is actually at the beach and also offers kayak rentals if you'd love to share this paddle with friends or family.

Kayak Wisconsin, Door County Peninsula

We head out to the two small specks of the Sister Islands on the horizon in a direct route to Porcupine Bay Road. We bypass the next two shoreline points–also called the Sister Bluffs, and head far out into Sister Bay. It is a hot summer day, and we cool down with paddle splash "fights". Great day for practicing wet exits (rolling over on purpose and practice finding the kayak skirt handle and pulling it off the cockpit to get out of the kayak while upside down), and then team rescues. We use the T rescue–the rescuer lines up his kayak in front of the victim's kayak to form a T, then pulls the victim's kayak up onto his lap—still upside down—to drain out the water while the person in the water holds on and helps stabilize the kayak, then flips the overturned kayak upright and positions the kayak parallel to his own kayak and leans over the now righted kayak to hold it while the wet one climbs up the back deck of the kayak and slides feet first into his cockpit and then rolls over into a sitting position. Practicing this maneuver makes it more likely it will be successful in a real rescue and is a great way to play in the water and cool off! Or, you could practice your kayak rolls or do half rolls by holding onto a partner's kayak.

If you choose to stay close to shore around the Sister Bluffs, then check out Little Sister Bay.

Bluffs, Beaches, Lighthouses and Shipwrecks

There is a great little public beach at the end of Pebble Beach Road in the southern end of the bay. Just north of the beach is an unidentified shipwreck of a wooden schooner south of the Little Sister Bay boat launch in 20 feet of water. Fun to look for. If you are hungry, then slip onto the beach at Fred and Fuzzy's Waterfront Bar and Grill at Little Sister Resort. It has a great outside eating area.

After your rest, paddle on into Sister Bay and head to the town. Sister Bay is actually the most populated town in Door County, but it doesn't feel like it. It has a nice sandy beach and kayak launch site. Al Johnson's Swedish restaurant with the goats on the roof is its most famous landmark, but Sister Bay offers a lot of other quiet spots to explore and enjoy. There is another quiet public access point at the north side of town at the end of Waters Edge Road. Bay Shore Outfitters now are also located in Sister Bay and offer kayak tours, rentals, lessons, and you could purchase a new kayak.

The Sister Islands are getting a bit larger as we paddle over the shipwreck of the schooner Meridan, who wrecked in 1873 in a howling fall storm when driving snow forced it off course and it sank off the south end of the Sister Islands in about 30-40 feet. There is a buoy to mark the

spot, we were not able to see much, as it is a little too deep to see.

The Sister Islands are designated a State Natural Area and are an important gullery and tern nesting area. We came around the west end of islands and surprised the millions–or so it seemed–birds on the island. It was like the movie "The Birds" come to life, except the birds were just surprised, not angry birds. It was really an awe inspiring spiritual moment. We just floated and marveled at the birds. The squawking and wings flapping just added to the whole wonderful hectic scene. You cannot land on the islands, nor would you want to, as the odor was as intense as the noise and movement!

After enjoying the islands and the birds, we headed towards the coast of Ellison Bluff and to Porcupine Bay, a very small inlet on the shore before the point. There we landed at Porcupine Bay Road public access which is by far one of our favorite public access sites. This fairly unknown area has big boulders perfect for our kitchen table, with an incredible view for our lunch. The beach is small rocks and felt like our own private beach for a cooling swim.

Logistics:

Directions to Kayak launches Peninsula State Park:

Off Shore Road:

45.1289, -87.2390. Enter the park off of Highway 42 at State Park Road by Fish Creek which turns into Shore Road. Immediately after the park headquarters turn left into the parking area. Long carry in access especially with low lake levels.

Weborg Point:

45.1339, -87.2404. Enter the park off of Highway 42 at State Park Road by Fish Creek which turns into Shore Road. Follow Shore Road for less than

Kayak Wisconsin, Door County Peninsula

1 mile to Weborg Point parking area. Shower and restrooms available.

Tennison Bay:

45.1619, -87.2350. Enter the park off of Highway 42 at State Park Road by Fish Creek which turns into Shore Road. Take a left and continue on Shore Road where it meets with Bluff Road. The kayak launch ramp is in the Tennison Bay Campground—turn left to the ramp by the shore. Restrooms are a significant walking distance from the launch.

Welckers Point:

45.1738, -87.2259. Enter the park off Highway 42 at State Park Road by Fish Creek which turns into Shore Road. Continue on Shore Road for about 3 miles to Welckers Point access road. Picnic area and restrooms.

Nicolet Boat Launch:

45.1687, -87.2226. Enter the park off Highway 42 onto Shore Road by Ephraim. Drive on Shore Road for a little more than 3 miles to the Boat Launch parking area. Pit toilets available.

Bluffs, Beaches, Lighthouses and Shipwrecks

Nicolet Beach Launch and kayak rentals:

45.1656, -87.2236. Enter the park off Highway 42 onto Shore Road by Ephraim. Drive on Shore Road for about 3 miles to the beach parking area. Showers and restrooms available.

Directions to Ephraim's Firehouse Marina:

45.1544, -87.1701. 9969 Water Street, Ephraim. Located on Highway 42 in downtown Ephraim. Restrooms available.

Directions to Ephraim Visitors Center Beach:

45.1589, -87.1722. 9877 Water Street, Ephraim. Located on Highway 42 in downtown Ephraim. Showers and restrooms and a drink machine available.

Directions to Pebble Beach Road beach:

45.1849,-87.1512. 10595 Pebble Beach Road, Little Sister Bay. From Highway 42, turn west just south of Sister Bay on Little Sister Hill Road, turn right onto Pebble Beach Road and follow it to the beach! No restrooms available.

Bluffs, Beaches, Lighthouses and Shipwrecks

Directions to Sister Bay Beach:

45.1899, -87.1219. 2362 Mill Road, Sister Bay. From Highway 42, turn onto Mill Road to the beach. Launch is at the southwest end of the beach. Restrooms available.

Directions to Waters End Road public access:

45.2074, -87.1207. From Highway 42, turn on Waters End Road towards the bay- just a short distance! No restrooms.

Directions to Porcupine Bay Road public access:

45.2446, -87.1121. From Highway 42, turn on Porcupine Bay Road towards the bay, travel about 1 ½ miles to the bay. There is a turnaround at the end of the road.

Shipwreck location:

Little Sister Bay unidentified wreck: 45.1856, -87.1508. Between Pebble Beach Road and Little Sister Resort in about 20 feet of water.

Kayak Wisconsin, Door County Peninsula

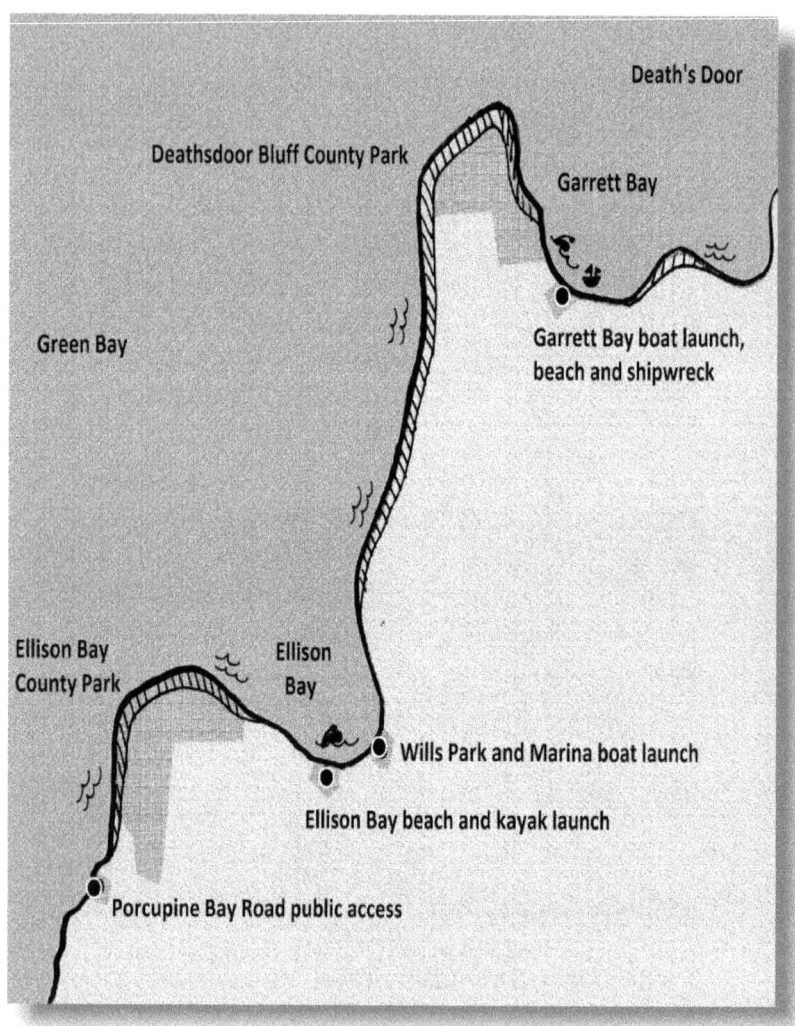

Leg 11

Tip of Door's Thumb

Sister Bay at Porcupine Bay Road to Garret Bay
With Ellison Bay and Bluff, Deathdoor Bluff, and a sunken ship
6 miles

Thumbs Up! 'Rounding the top of the Door Peninsula is one of our top picks (like the pun?) for a day paddle as we circumnavigate Wisconsin's fun thumb. It definitely is a "thumbs up" paddle as it encompasses two of the best headlands–Ellison Bluff and Deathdoor Bluff, fantastic lake art, and the high probability of seeing a sunken ship! It may also have an increase in challenges as the paddle starts out in the bay of Green Bay where the Door County land mass may provide calmer seas in the lee, but when rounding Deathdoor Bluff the protection ends and the change in wind and waves may be surprising.

Although it is not a long paddle it would be possible to cut it into two paddles. Porcupine Bay Road public access to Ellison Bay's Women's Center Beach is about a 2 mile paddle, and Ellison Bay to the Garret Bay kayak launch is about 4 miles.

Kayak Wisconsin, Door County Peninsula

Porcupine Bay Road is one of our favorite public access sites as it is open, airy and sparkling. The mini Porcupine Bay shoreline is small rocks. As soon as you enter the water and head towards the tip you can't miss the 100 foot high limestone Ellison Bluff. The bluff is part of the Ellison Bluff County Park and you are free to land below the bluff and enjoy the view up. You may see hikers at the top of the bluff enjoying the view down as this county park is known to have one of the best views of all Green Bay and has an observation deck along with a catwalk that extends out over the bluff!

Rounding Ellison Bay bluff takes you into Ellison Bay and towards the town of Ellison Bay. Here is where you will find the public Women's Center

Bluffs, Beaches, Lighthouses and Shipwrecks

Beach and kayak launch site for Ellison Bay. It is inside of the bay at the south side, head for the south side of the long pier and look for the picnic gazebo above to help find it. The kayak launch is on the rocky south side of the pier and the sandy beach on the north side of the pier is for swimmers only. Just a speck north in the bay is Wills Park and Marina which has a boat ramp for public use and little picnic area which is another spectacular spot to relax and watch the sun set over the bay.

Ellison Bay was founded in 1866 by Johan Eliason who came from Denmark. Ellison Bay is part of Door County's north area where the crowds have thinned and it's easier to slow down and marvel at nature's exquisite beauty. We recommend staying in one of the areas quaint inns with small town charm and hospitality where the innkeepers are delighted to share their local knowledge to enhance your Door Peninsula experience. We have stayed in almost every town in the area and have always found the innkeepers supportive of kayakers and our kayak trailer. Door County obviously prides itself on their vintage inns and resorts!

Next, aim your kayak towards the next imposing headland with the scary name: Deathdoor Bluff. 'Kind of looks like a jet crashing into the bay,

Kayak Wisconsin, Door County Peninsula

which does befit its name. Deathdoor Bluff is another great viewpoint for sunset vistas with a trail to the bluff and lookout high above Green Bay. This is again an exceptional county park and you absolutely should stop below the bluff to enjoy the lake art and perhaps add one yourself! We were amazed by the unique creativity and rock balancing ability of the "artists". 'Gave it a try. . .our lowly small stone cairns not even close to the grandeur of the artists. . .anyone offer classes on lake art? Search for the Potawatomi Pictographs hidden in Deathsdoor Bluff Park. Exact location is a well kept secret to protect them, but that makes it more exciting if you do find them.

Bluffs, Beaches, Lighthouses and Shipwrecks

Deathdoor Bluff is where a major Indian battle took place between the Potawatomi and Winnebago Nations and may be the actual origin of the term "Port de Mort" or Death's Door. In the 1640's the Potawatomi had been forced westward and started to settle in Wisconsin and Door County where the Winnebago's already lived. The Potawatomi's came across Death's Door in canoes (a feat in itself) from Washington Island to fight the Winnebago's but were repelled by the Winnebago warriors who fought from the top of the 100 foot high Deathdoor bluff. Looking up at the bluff it is easy to imagine arrows raining down on us as we round the point.

The view of Washington Island seven miles away impressively dominates the horizon because it is the largest of the six Potawatomi Islands off the coast of the Door Peninsula. The other five circle around Washington Island with Plum Island being the closest to the peninsula and the long sleek Detroit Island behind it. The ones we cannot see from this vantage point are little Pilot Island with its lighthouse and cormorants forming a triangle off of the tip of Detroit Island, then tiny Hog Island hidden off the eastern side of Washington Island, and the state park Rock Island the most northern of the Potawatomi Islands which is north of Washington Island.

Kayak Wisconsin, Door County Peninsula

Off the tip of Deathdoor Bluff is some of the best salmon fishing in Door County. Look down and see if you can spy a salmon. The King or Chinook salmon is long with a black mouth and gums with a square tail with spots all over it, the Coho salmon is smaller with white gums and a black mouth and it has a forked tail with spots only on the top, and the Atlantic salmon has a short face, smaller mouth and forked tail. Salmon are in the same family as trout, but whereas salmon are more pointed and slender, trout tend to be more round. Wisconsin trout include steelhead, brook, brown and rainbow. Brook trout are native to Wisconsin, but most of the other salmon and trout are stocked in the Great Lakes–your fishing license supports this. OK, you probably won't really see one by looking down as they tend to swim in deep water. But, fishing salmon from a kayak could be an interesting proposition...

Deathdoor Bluff ties Table Bluff as the most northerly points of the Door Peninsula, so we are truly rounding the tip of the thumb as we cruise on into Garret Bay. This side of Hedgehog Harbor is the quiet side with limited motor boat activity. As you get closer to the boat landing–look down! The 1867 Schooner Fleetwing fell victim to Death's Door and was lost in a gale in 1888. The

Fleetwing is only 110-500 feet northeast of the boat landing and is only five to twenty-five feet down–one of the best opportunities to actually see a shipwreck from a kayak.

The Garret Bay kayak launch is a public beach, so go ahead and swim out to the shipwreck to explore. Better yet bring along your snorkeling gear for the best views, just don't touch the artifacts. There is a quiet picnic area in the woods by the boat launch, or just sit by the water and enjoy the view of Washington Island.

Logistics:

Directions to Porcupine Bay Road public access:

45.2446, -87.1132. From highway 42 south of Ellison Bay, turn west on Porcupine Bay Road and follow it about 1 ¼ miles until it dead ends at bay.

Directions to The Women's Center – Ellison Bay kayak launch:

45.2530, -87.0776. As you enter Ellison Bay from the south on Highway 42 look to the left for the sign "Women's Center" and turn down the hill on Bayview Road that leads to the Ellison Bay beach and kayak launch.

Directions to Wills Park and Marina:

45.2547,-87.0746. 12033 Cedar Shore Road, Ellison Bay. From Highway 42 in Ellison Bay, turn west on Cedar Shore Road for a short distance to the marina and public boat launch. Launch fee.

Directions to Garret Bay boat launch beach:

45.2859, -87.0512. From Highway 42, turn onto Garret Bay Road for 2.3 miles. The boat launch is on the left when you first see Garret Bay.

Shipwreck location:

Fleetwing: 45.2858, -87.0504. 100-500 feet northeast of the Garret Bay boat launch.

Kayak Wisconsin, Door County Peninsula

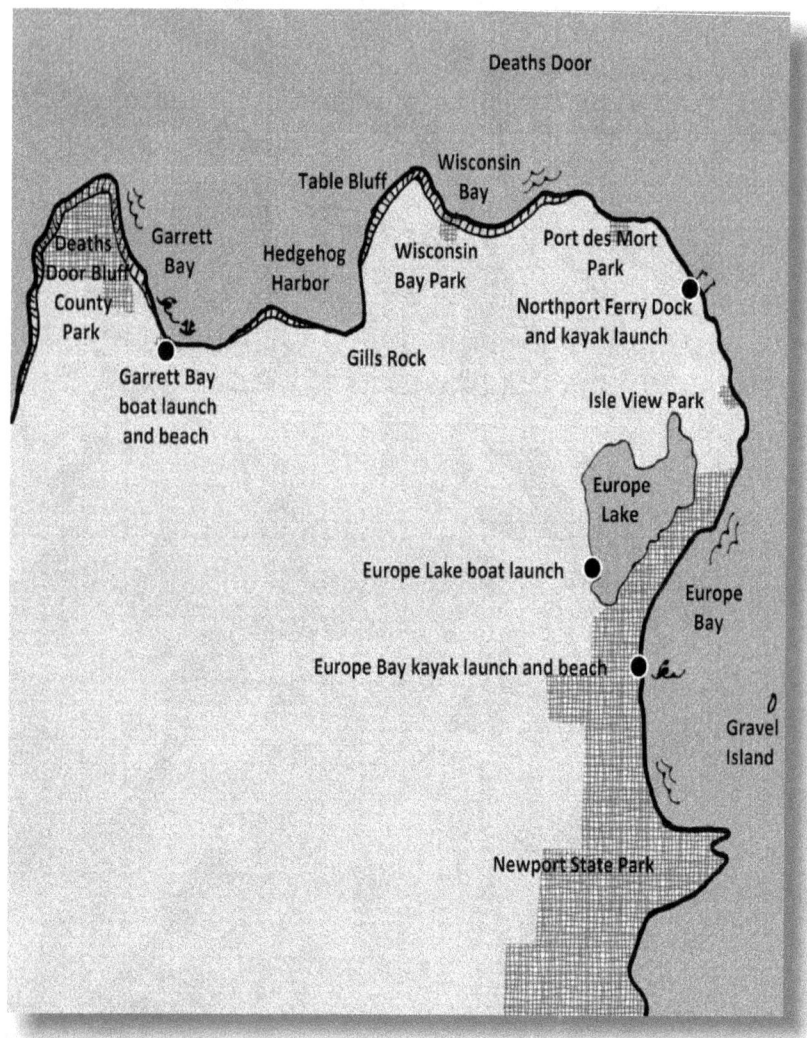

Leg 12

Deaths Door

Garret Bay to Northport to Europe Bay on Lake Michigan
With quaint Gills Rock, Table Bluff, views of Washington Island and Newport State Park
7 miles

Death's Door. . .sounds so ominous; who knew it could be so beautiful? This paddle definitely has the WOW factor with Gills Rock—a quaint fishing village with the Maritime Museum, Table Bluff headland, Wisconsin Bay with the best view of Washington Island and the ferry boats, and finally out of Green Bay and into Lake Michigan with it's incredible expansive view and on the shoreline Wisconsin's only wilderness park–Newport State Park with its pristine coast. Every way you look there are hard to believe views. Some people pay good money for this.

If you want to take more time and savor the tip of the Wisconsin's thumb and Death's Door, you could divide this paddle into two paddles: 5 miles from Garret's Bay boat landing to the east side of Northport's Harbor, and then about 2 miles from there to Europe Bay boat landing, all along Newport State Park shoreline.

Kayak Wisconsin, Door County Peninsula

We are all alone for this paddle, just Rick, Chris and myself. We planned on doing this leg by itself, but the weather forecast for the day we scheduled it called for 70% chance of thunderstorms, high winds, and a small craft advisory. . .which may have discouraged family and friends from joining us on our adventure through Deaths Door, where the treacherous waters of Lake Michigan clash with the waters of Green Bay and many shipwrecks are the result. With the weather a bit edgy, 'did seem like it might be pushing our luck just a wee bit, so we chose to add this paddle onto Leg 11's and do it on the same beautiful day.

Take your time slipping into the water at Garret's Bay Boat Landing as the shipwreck of the Schooner Fleetwing is just northeast of the boat landing and only 5 to 25 feet underwater. True to the Death's Door legacy the Fleetwing crashed on shore in a storm in 1888. Take some time to enjoy the Garret Bay's rocky beach and either swim out to the sunken ship or kayak above it.

Continue paddling across Hedgehog Harbor towards the small picturesque fishing village of Gills Rock–known as the tip of the thumb. Visit the town for the Door County Maritime Museum which has lots of artifacts from the shipwrecks in Deaths Door and around the peninsula. Passenger

Bluffs, Beaches, Lighthouses and Shipwrecks

ferries to Washington Island also come and go from Gills Rock. The Shoreline Restaurant has great fresh perch and wonderful views, and Charlie's Smokehouse offers Lake Michigan smoked salmon and whitefish.

Gills Rock was originally called "Hedgehog Harbor" when Amos, a Washington Island fisherman kept his sloop in the cove over a winter in 1855. A family of hedgehogs chewed holes into the boat's hull, which he apparently did not notice, and Mr. Lovejoy was forced to abandon his sloop and come ashore. Thankfully the town was renamed Gills Rock in honor of a prominent lumberer. Why it's called Gills "Rock" instead of Gills "town" we are not quite sure of, since no big rock in town is noticeable from the harbor.

However, the point past Gills Rock is a big rock, but it is not called Gills "Rock", it is known as Table Bluff. This is such a beautiful area that I made it my book cover! As you head towards the bluff, watch for the ferry boats that come steaming through here. Remember the old adage "the right of way"–it very much applies to kayaking–if the boat is on your right, they have the right of way, if the boat is on your left–you have the right of way, but in a small kayak, we give all boats the right of way!

Kayak Wisconsin, Door County Peninsula

Paddle around Table Bluff into Wisconsin Bay. It is a pretty bay with an obviously wonderful name. In Wisconsin Bay there are a couple of private docks, then shoreline, and then a couple more private docks. In the middle of the bay between the docks is Wisconsin Bay Park. Depending on water levels, you can land under the park bluff. As you round the next little point, there is another small park, Port Des Morts Park. Both would be impressive places to stop for a picnic on the rock shelf under the bluffs and a leisurely view of the islands off the tip of Death's Door Peninsula.

We are now smack dab in the middle of Death's Door. It is the narrow strait between the tip of the thumb of Wisconsin's Peninsula and Washington Island. We always thought that the name came from the many shipwrecks located here, but the name is actually attributed to Jean Nicolet, the French missionary, who wrote it as "Porte des Morts", Door of Death. But he actually got that name from the oral history of the Native Americans living on the Peninsula. The name Death's Door may have originated from the battle between the Potawatomi and Winnebago (Ho-Chunk) Native Americans that was fought here in the strait and on Deathdoor Bluff, back on the bay side of the Peninsula. The Native Americans lost hundreds of warriors in the battle. But it could also be called Deaths Door due the sudden loss of over 10,000 Winnebago people from 1634 to 1650. No one knows for sure the cause of all the deaths.

What is clear, is that Death's Door has lived up to its name, as it may have more shipwrecks than any other section of fresh water in the world! Therefore, it does behoove us to be aware that the waters of Green Bay clash with the waters of Lake Michigan, and they don't play well together, as the strait is famous for dangerous currents and waves. Unless you'd like to join the mystique, always check and recheck the weather forecast before venturing into the door of death. . .

Our paddle has taken us from the calm waters of the lee in Green Bay around the tip into a slight wind that was still capable of creating one footers and making us paddle into the wind. As we paddle around the last of the tip of Door's thumb we come to the small town of Northport that is the terminus for the ferry dock of Washington Island. It is a very busy harbor in the summer, and there is not much time between the departure and then arrival of the next ferry. This could be your take out spot if want more time to gaze at views. The kayak launch is on the east side of the harbor. The Northport Pier Restaurant offers food with a view.

Rounding the Northport harbor brings us squarely into Lake Michigan and now the small waves and wind are at our side with small whitecaps, so it is important to know how to brace as the whitecaps roll from the side. A kayak skirt and the PFD (personal floatation device, a "lifejacket") are essential.

About a half mile after Northport is one more of the many small Liberty Grove township parks, Isle View Park. Gee, wonder why they named it that? The park is above on the bluff, but you may land on the beach and sit and enjoy the island views with the layers of jade green floating on the azure blue of Lake Michigan. You are as close as

Bluffs, Beaches, Lighthouses and Shipwrecks

you can be to Pilot Island and its lighthouse, unless you choose to paddle the almost three miles east out to it, but beware it is national wildlife sanctuary and the cormorants love the place. . .and the grounds are not even open to explore. But, you also have a fantastic view of Plum Island two miles north and the now automated range lights on this island. Plum Island is also a National Wildlife Sanctuary and is now open to the public to explore its forest, shoreline and migratory birds. One and a half miles behind these two wildlife refuge lighthouse islands is the long, sleek private Detroit Island, then looming behind Detroit Island is massive Washington Island.

Venturing back out along the shoreline, within another half mile we are paddling past Newport State Park, Wisconsin's only wilderness park. The park has eleven miles of shoreline, and this section is Europe Bay Woods and is a neck of land between inland Europe Lake and Lake Michigan. This isthmus of beaches and dunes was once the ancient shoreline of Lake Michigan. Europe Lake does have a boat launch and is a wonderful choice for kayaking if Green Bay and Lake Michigan wave action are a little too rough. The eastern shore of Europe Lake is part of Newport State Park.

Kayak Wisconsin, Door County Peninsula

We are heading into Europe Bay, the first bay on the Lake Michigan side. When we are in sight of Gravel Island, an additional national wildlife refuge, then it's time to turn into shore for Europe Bay Road, a designated kayak takeout/launch. The bay becomes shallow but is a nice swimming beach if you are willing to walk out a ways. The view is incredible–overlooking the great expanse of Lake Michigan, since the Michigan side of Lake Michigan is about 118 miles away, way past the horizon, all you can see is brilliant blue! Time to rest and embrace the quiet lapping of the waves and soak up the pastel blue sky and sapphire blue waters.

Logistics:

Directions to Garret Bay boat launch and beach:

45.2860, -87.0511. From Highway 42, turn onto Garret Bay Road for 2.3 miles. The boat launch is on the left when you first see Garret Bay.

Directions to Wisconsin Bay Park:

45.2953, -87.0097. 742 Wisconsin Bay Road. From Highway 42 turn north on Wisconsin Bay Road where it intersects with Wisconsin Bay Road and Timberline Road. Go north and the park is on the bay at the first curve to the left. On a bluff-not a kayak launch site.

Directions to Port des Morts Park:

45.2956, -86.9864. From Highway 42, right before it ends at Northport, turn north on Kenosha Road. The park is at the end of the road at the water's edge where Lake Michigan meets Green Bay. On a bluff, not a kayak launch site.

Directions to Northport kayak launch:

45.2902, -86.9769. Couldn't be any easier. Take Highway 42 north until it ends at the ferry dock. Look to the east side of the harbor for the kayak launch.

Directions to Isle View Park:

45.2819, -86.9721. From Highway 42 north, a little more than 1 mile south of Gills Rock, turn east on Isle View Road. Drive approximately 2 ½ miles east and when Isle View Road ends at Northern Door Road you will find the entrance to the small Isle View Park. Picnic and grill area, if you are ambitious you may climb down to the water's edge.

Directions to Europe Bay Kayak takeout/launch:

45.2594, -86.9851. Take Highway 42 north past the town of Ellison Bay, and when the highway turns north towards Northport—stay straight on Europe Bay Road and follow it to its end at Europe Bay on Lake Michigan. Don't be confused–the area seems to have several a.k.a.'s : Liberty Grove Town Park or Hotz County Park. There are pit toilets available but no running water.

Bluffs, Beaches, Lighthouses and Shipwrecks

Directions to the Door County Maritime Museum at Gills Rock:

45.2921, -87.0216. 12724 W. Wisconsin Bay Road, Ellison Bay. From Highway 42, right after it turns west at Gills Rock, turn north on Wisconsin Bay Road at tug boat Skipper on display. The museum is the first building on the right.

Shipwreck location:

Fleetwing: 45.2858, -87.0504. 100-500 feet northeast of the Garret Bay boat launch.

Kayak Wisconsin, Door County Peninsula

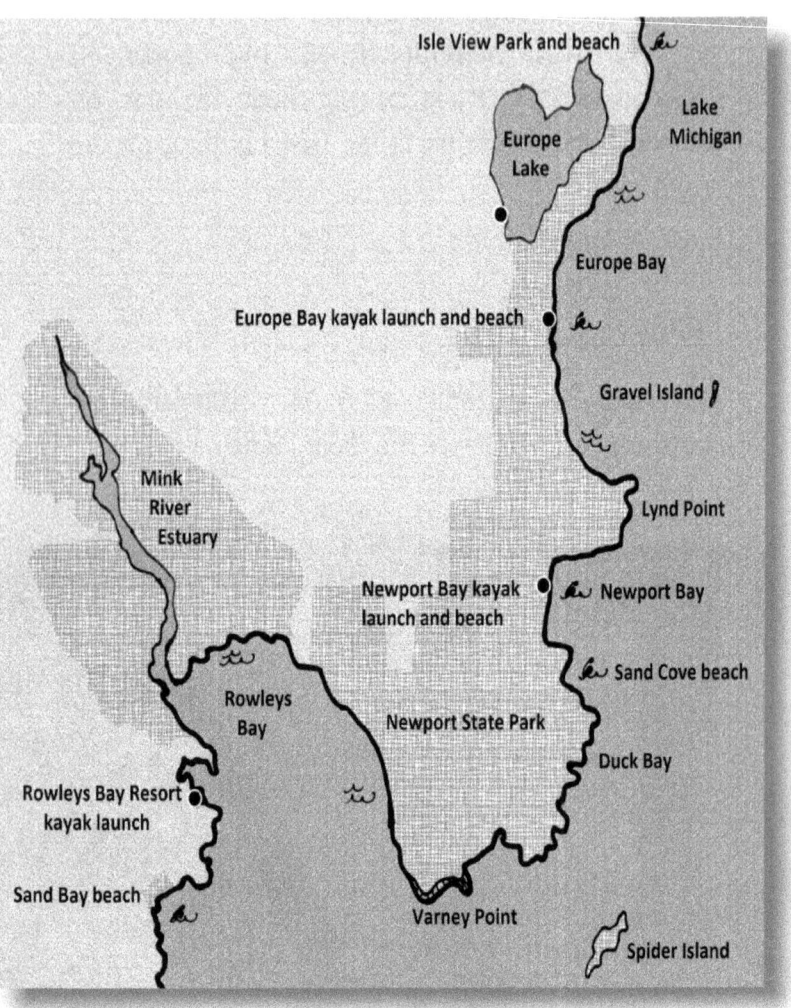

Leg 13

The Wilderness

Europe Bay to Mink River Estuary and Rowleys Bay

With nature lover's Newport State Park and the Mink River Estuary

10 miles

"Goin' Up North" or seeing Wisconsin's "God's Country"–this paddle is a nature lover's dream. This is a tour of Newport State Park's true wilderness shoreline and the unspoiled Mink River Estuary. There are oodles of wildlife to search and discover on this paddle.

Now that we are kayaking the Lake Michigan side of the Peninsula, we generally have switched the direction of our paddles and are paddling south to north due to the wind and wave action. We did this leg as two paddles to genuinely enjoy the coast line and the estuary. Our first from Rowleys Bay Resort kayak launch into the bowl of the bay and down into the Mink River Estuary and back (there is a hiking/portage kayak launch in the Mink River but ¾ of a mile seems like too much work. . .). This is a 5 mile paddle depending on how deep into the Mink River you go, and the second from Rowley's Bay Resort kayak launch to Europe Bay about 5 miles.

To explore the Mink River Estuary you can put in at Rowleys Bay Resort which does have a marina that is public, and has a specific kayak launch area, so you can skip the busy one lane ramp launch in the marina. DC Adventures Center is located here, so you can bring the whole gang and all rent kayaks, or if you don't feel ready to tackle the waves on your own, join one of their kayak tours. Take out one of their SUP's, a stand up paddleboard, for a loftier view down into the bay water–gives you a whole new perspective! We found the DC Adventure guides extremely helpful in sharing weather conditions and directions to the Mink River mouth.

Rowleys Bay Resort is the location of Rutabaga's Sea Kayak Symposium, an annual summer event filled with kayak tours, classes, workshops, exhibits, and presentations. It's all about sea kayaking and exploring the Door Peninsula in a group environment. Consider this opportunity to learn novel techniques and gain new friends.

For our day tour, leave the resort and marina turn left, north, and head into the bowl of the bay and towards the Mink River. We explored the Mink River Estuary in late fall and shared Rowleys Bay

Bluffs, Beaches, Lighthouses and Shipwrecks

with geese hunters. They are hard to spot at times as they lay in camouflaged boats, generally very quietly... We whispered past them as we hugged the shoreline to stay clear of rustling up birds near them. This did keep us close to the shallows of the bay and the rocky shoreline with breakers.

Once in the Mink River, all is calm and peaceful. It is an estuary because the hard spring fed river water flows into and mixes with Lake Michigan's softer waters. It is a rare enduring estuary, one of the few still existing in the US. The Mink River is pristine, never touched since the Potawatomi people roamed here a century ago. You can float and check out the rare plants, birds and wildlife.

Kayak Wisconsin, Door County Peninsula

There are 200 species of birds that migrate through the estuary each year—good luck at finding them all, kind of like a nature's "Where's Waldo". You are totally hidden in the grasses, lake irises, and dune thistle as they get closer and closer until you finally admit you have gone as far as you can. Then the fun is in attempting to turn around to head back out!

Take your time heading back out, you might see a few more of the many birds and more wildlife. Kayaking the Mink River Estuary is a very popular tour as it is more inland and less open water paddling and therefore a good beginner kayaking trip. So instead of doing this one as Leg 13, perhaps it should have been our first leg...

We did the Rowleys Bay to Europe Bay paddle in summer. Again, start at Rowleys Bay Resort, or just continue north as you leave the Mink River Estuary. We stopped and camped at Varney Point in Newport State Park. Don't you wonder who Varney is?–maybe he is Barney's cousin? Actually the Varney family sold this point for inclusion into the park. Newport is Wisconsin's only wilderness park and the only wilderness camping you can legally do in Door County. Well worth our effort. We ended up the only campers on Varney Point even though there are three wilderness campsites on the point. They are far enough apart, that it would be fine to share, but we were alone for our night's stay. Our favorite part was when the clouds cleared and the stars came out. We sat on the bluff at the point and star gazed the entire sparkly Milky Way!

Just remember to call Newport State Park office when you arrive at your reserved campsite. Yup, you generally do have cell phone service in most of Door County as we discovered. . . Otherwise, kind residents of Door County notice that no one has returned to their vehicle over night and become worried, and when they become worried then they call the police, and then the police start calling family members, and then you have many scared family members leaving umpteen messages on your phones wondering if you are lost at sea, and then you need to call all said family members to calm them down, and call Officer Troy and explain your mistake, and hope that no Coast Guard search and rescue missions were sent out. All in all, we felt pretty dumb, but were really happy to know that Door County residents SINCERELY care about the tourists that visit them.

While we were oblivious to everyone's concern, we were enjoying Varney Point and its great view of Spider Island, and this could be another paddle to explore the island by boat. You can't land however, as Spider Island, along with Gravel Island off of Europe Bay are National Wildlife Refuges for a breeding ground for native and migratory birds. It is one of the smallest wilderness areas in the country.

We bathed and swam in the clean waters off the point with our environmentally friendly soap—could have skinny dipped since we were all alone in our own 307 mile long and 118 mile wide private Lake Michigan "bathtub". Lake Michigan is the only Great Lake that we do not share with Canada and is the fifth largest lake in the world, and it seemed like it was all ours!

Finally we said goodbye to our privacy, packed up our campsite, left no trace, and clambered back into our kayaks and continued our adventure north along Newport's eleven miles of shoreline. Story goes that Newport was a thriving lumber town, logged to rebuild Chicago after their great fire. Now Newport is not only a nature lovers dream for kayaking but it also offers 2,400 acres of wilderness with thirty miles of hiking trails, twelve miles of biking trails and sixteen backpack in or kayak to wilderness campsites. And Door County is not only for summer, come in winter for

Newport's eight miles of snowshoe trails or twenty three miles of cross country skiing.

Back to our summer day beneath a bountiful blue sky, shimmering off the clear turquoise waters of Lake Michigan. A quiet day for paddling with some breakers around the rocky points, so you do need to give a wide berth around the points and into Duck Bay's shallow bay, we did see some ducks so maybe that's why it's called Duck Bay?

Then around the big point of Newport State Park into Sand Cove and Newport Bay. There is a kayak launch and swimming beach in Newport Bay, perfect for a beach picnic on our exquisite sunny day.

Kayak Wisconsin, Door County Peninsula

We continued on around Lynd Point, again–who is Lynd? And then into Europe Bay, another aqua blue bay that is very shallow. We took out at the same spot as Leg 12's at the end of Europe Bay Road which is another great Liberty Grove Town Park–Hotz Memorial Town Park (still part of Newport State Park). Ferdinand Hotz was a wealthy Chicago jeweler who once owned 1400 acres, most of which he never developed, of what is now Newport State Park. Not quite sure why the park has so many names, but it is a wonderful spot for relaxing and having a picnic, or lounging on a blanket on the beach, or swim and cool off after a day of paddling or. . .

<u>Logistics</u>

Directions to Rowleys Bay Resort boat landing and kayak launch:

45.2197, -87.0340. 1041 County Road ZZ, Ellison Bay. From Highway 42, just north of where Highway 57 ends/connects to Highway 42 by in the town of Sister Bay, turn east on County Road ZZ and follow it while it twists and turns (first north, then east) to Rowley Bay and the resort. Continue past the marina to a small road to the left for the kayak launch

Bluffs, Beaches, Lighthouses and Shipwrecks

Directions to Newport Bay kayak launch in Newport State Park:

45.2378, -86.9852. From Highway 42 north of Ellison Bay, turn south on County NP and follow it as it curves east. When County NP comes to a T intersection, continue following NP by turning right/south on Newport Lane and continue into Newport State Park on Newport Park Road and follow it until it ends at a parking lot. You will need to carry your kayaks 500 feet to the shoreline. There is the State Park fee, restrooms available.

Directions to Europe Bay Kayak launch in Newport State Park:

45.2594, -86.9851. Take Highway 42 north past the town of Ellison Bay, and when the highway turns north towards Northport–stay straight on Europe Bay Road and follow it to its end at the Europe Bay on Lake Michigan. This is part of Newport State Park, so you do need a state park sticker or pay the daily fee. There are pit toilets available but no running water.

Kayak Wisconsin, Door County Peninsula

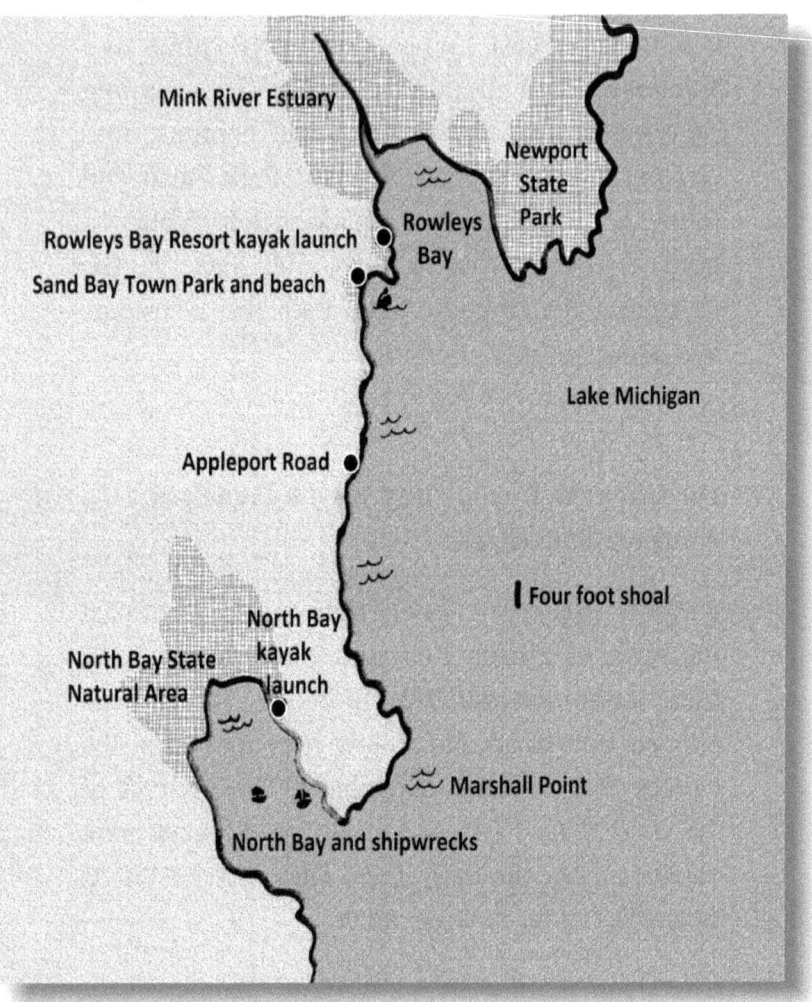

Leg 14

The Wild Side

Rowleys Bay to North Bay
*With North Bay Natural Area and
Sand Bay Beach and two century old shipwrecks*
9 miles

Rain, rain, go away. . . Shopping? Kayaking? Decisions, decisions. Ultimately, the forecast changed from 70% storms to clearing by midday. Kayaking! The Wild Side paddle has a double meaning–there are several wild natural areas on this paddle and the Lake Michigan side of the Door Peninsula is often the wilder, more challenging kayaking side during the summer. But for 'weathering' the conditions or enjoying paddle surfing of white caps, you are rewarded with a sweet sandy beach in the small Sand Bay as you head into Rowleys Bay. And add on the "gives me chills" to discover the 100+ years old shipwrecks in North Bay!

We launched at North Bay to head north as the summer winds work best that way towards Rowleys Bay. You could shorten this paddle to 5 miles at Appleport Road which dead ends at the lake, or continue paddling to Sand Bay Town Park for an 8 mile paddle. Appleport Road to Rowleys

Kayak Wisconsin, Door County Peninsula

Bay Resort is about 3 miles and from Sand Bay Town Park to Rowleys Bay Resort boat landing is just one more mile.

There used to be two kayak launches in North Bay. One was at the end of Winding Lane—sounds so nice doesn't it? But as luck would have it, the lake levels have dropped and the boat launch is now a half mile walk to actually get to water. Skip this access and head to the North Bay boat landing–which now is only usable by small watercraft.

The North Bay Road kayak launch is very shallow for a longggggg way, but has a small channel dug out so head straight out into the bay rather than angling up the bay coast. Inside this quiet bay lies the North Bay State Natural Area. It has many shallow cold water springs and Three Springs Creek drain into North Bay through a marsh. This area encourages spawning of northern pike, perch, bass, salmon and trout. The marsh has a variety of grasses, cattail and the dwarf lake iris and some rare orchids. The shorebirds are fun to watch as we glide out into the bay.

Our first excitement is the Cherubusco sunken shipwreck. Angle across the bay toward the south point and keep the boat launch straight behind you. About a quarter of the way across the bay

and at about halfway out of the bay, start looking down and treasure hunt for this three masted barque ship which sailed with square rigging. The Cherubusco was stranded in North Bay by a November storm in 1874. She lies upright and intact but mostly buried in the golden sand with her centerboard and sides visible. Her bow points to the mouth of the bay.

After discovering the Cherubusco, head to the north point of the bay, and before Marshall Point, there is an L shaped private dock within a little cove. Here lies the Boaz shipwreck. She was a three masted schooner built in Sheboygan and stranded in the bay in 1900. The Boaz lies broken in 10 feet of water with her two centerboard trunks upright. Seek, sightsee, and enjoy these protected Wisconsin heritage treasures.

After shipwreck hunting, we start rounding Marshall Point on the north side of the bay which is a gated natural preserve with private homes on the shoreline. It is here that we meet the whole front of Lake Michigan with rough conditions in the rocky shallows. Lake Michigan is a waterway system that is linked to the Mississippi River and the Gulf of Mexico, and the lake drains into Lake Huron on its way to the Atlantic Ocean. As we get the full effect of Lake Michigan, we think someone must have pulled the plug! We are pushed by two foot water waves with occasional three footers (you can tell a three footer because you lose sight of your partners who sit about 3 feet tall in a kayak). We actually get to surf the swells and start having a 'swell' time.

We round the northern end of Marshall Point which gives us a bit of protection. There are roaring white caps on the shoreline and four foot crashing waves over Four Foot Shoal to our starboard, right side in Lake Michigan. Four Foot Shoal is considered one of the best places to catch king salmon, trout and northern pike in Lake Michigan, but today, there are no fishermen braving the conditions as the wind started changing directions and the lake became choppy and confused–or maybe that was just us. . .

Up the coast is Appleport Road which dead ends at the lake and could be your take out spot. Then before the little point is Sand Bay and the small Sand Bay Town Park, known for its–aw, you guessed it–sandy beach. Sand Bay Town Park is a great spot for a bathroom break or a picnic lunch and is a designated kayak launch site.

After the point past Sand Bay begin rounding into Rowleys Bay. Rowleys Bay is the Bay opposite Ellison Bay on the Green Bay side. If you stop and look at the Door Peninsula map, you will notice that almost every bay on the Lake Michigan side, has a corresponding bay on the Green Bay side. Actually, the Mink River in the bowl of Rowleys Bay makes it more than half way to Ellison Bay before petering out in the beautiful estuary.

In 1680, Father Andre, a Jesuit priest landed in Rowleys Bay to start a mission, however he didn't get the bay named after him. That distinction goes to Peter Rowley who left the congestion of Fort Howard in Green Bay to settle at this point, but didn't stay long as he started feeling crowded even here. Really??!!

Kayak Wisconsin, Door County Peninsula

We head into the bay and to the public boat landing and marina at Rowleys Resort. The kayak launch is next to a pier before the marina. Relax on the shoreline and enjoy the view. Most of Rowleys Bay shoreline is natural area preserves–gaze into the bay and the pristine, never been touched, Mink River Estuary and then slowly scan across Rowleys Bay to Varney Point in Newport State Park—the only wilderness state park in all of Wisconsin.

You might want to stop into Grandma's Swedish Bakery at the resort for a delicious, gigantic sticky pecan roll or a savory onion bialys, a mix of an English muffin and a bagel. Or stay for Rowleys

Bluffs, Beaches, Lighthouses and Shipwrecks

Resort's all you can eat Fish Boil with its sky high flaming conclusion just when it's ready to eat.

We had a great time staying in our yurt at the Wagon Trail Campground. The round Mongolian tent has lattice support walls and a domed roof with a skylight. A fun step up from camping and we enjoyed looking for our yurt key, who has the yurt key??

Logistics:

Directions to North Bay Boat Launch:

45.1514, -87.0610. From Highway 42, just north of where Highway 57 meets 42 at Sister Bay, turn east on Highway ZZ, go about 2 ¼ miles and turn south on North Bay Road. Travel about 2 miles on North Bay Road and follow it as it turns into a gravel road down to the North Bay boat launch.

Directions to Appleport Road:

45.1856, -87.0421. From Highway 42, just north of where Highway 57 meets 42 at Sister Bay, turn east on Highway ZZ, go about 2 ½ miles, when ZZ turns north—continue straight on Appleport Road until it dead ends at Lake Michigan.

Kayak Wisconsin, Door County Peninsula

Directions to Sand Bay Town Park

45.2122, -87.0400. 11154 N. Sand Bay Lane. From Highway 42 at the north end of Sister Bay, turn east on Waters End Road, travel about 3 miles across the peninsula. Then turn north on Sand Bay Lane to the park.

Directions to Rowleys Bay State Boat Access:

45.2193, -87.0341. 1041 County Road ZZ. From Highway 42, just north of where Highway 57 meets 42 at Sister Bay, turn east on Highway ZZ, travel about 3 ½ miles to Rowleys Bay Resort and the State Boat Access area. The kayak launch is past the marina and the DC Adventures building, turn left down the gravel road, the launch is next to the pier.

<u>**Shipwreck locations:**</u>

Cherubusco: 45.1417, -87.0621. Middle north side of North Bay in about 10 feet of water.

Boaz: 45.1390, -87.0514. North Bay, near Marshall Point in a little cove by a private L shaped dock in 10 feet of water.

Kayak Wisconsin, Door County Peninsula

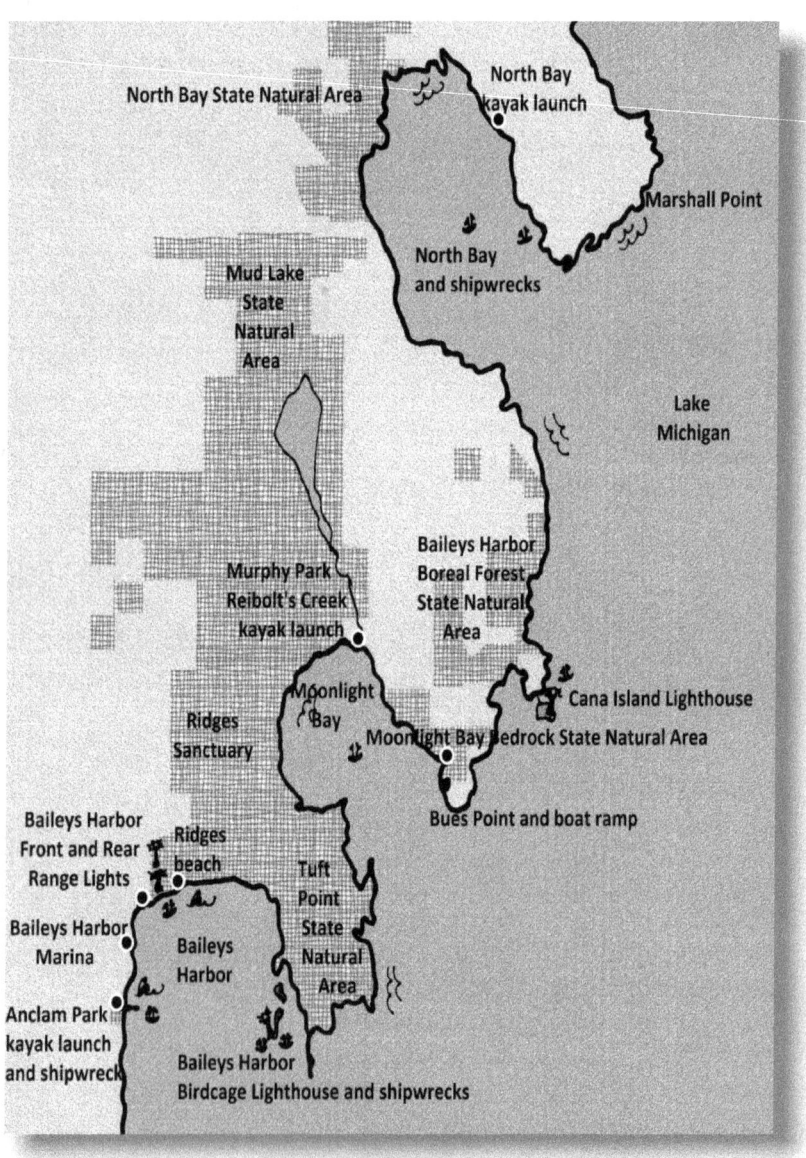

Leg 15

Lighthouses

North Bay to Baileys Harbor

With Cana Island Lighthouse, Moonlight Bay, Bailey Harbor Lighthouse, and mega shipwrecks
10.5 miles

Ship Ahoy! There are eleven lighthouses around the mainland and islands of the Door Peninsula. This paddle offers four of the most popular and unique lighthouses: Cana Island and Lighthouse, Baileys Harbor birdcage Lighthouse, and the Front and Rear Baileys Harbor Range Lights. But this paddle doesn't end there, no way, there are tons of natural pristine nature, the "must see" Ridges Sanctuary and Beach, Toft Point Natural Area, Moonlight Bay Bedrock Beach Natural Area, Baileys Harbor Boreal Forest Area and an entire Cana Island to roam. And if you love searching for shipwrecks, this is the paddle for you. Whew!

'A speck over our 10 mile limit, but can be cut in half almost exactly at Bues Point Boat Landing. We launched at Anclam Park, but Baileys Harbor also has several other possibilities for launching kayaks: the large downtown Bailey Harbor Marina, or just a wee bit down the road off Ridges

Kayak Wisconsin, Door County Peninsula

Road at Lake View Road Park, or Ridges Sanctuary Beach. Ridges Sanctuary, across the road from its beach, is considered one of the "must see" places in Wisconsin, famous for 26 species of rare orchids native to Wisconsin.

This was one of our most technical paddles. There is the old adage for the Lake Michigan coast line on the Door Peninsula–"winds from the south—don't go". . .and guess what—the winds were from the south, but at a manageable 10 knots, so we gave it a go. To not work against the wind, we chose to paddle south to north and put in at Anclam Park in Baileys Harbor and headed northwest up the coast to the North Bay Boat Launch, now only usable for shallow watercraft.

Baileys Harbor was discovered in 1848 by Captain Bailey when he took refuge from an autumn storm in the little inlet. The natural limestone and the abundance of trees convinced him to encourage his boss into building a business in the harbor. Within two years there was a pier, sawmill and a stone quarry in Baileys Harbor and the town was begun.

Anclam Park is a little town park at the south end of Baileys Harbor. The jetty is the remnants of an old pier used by John Anclam's business for supplies and timber in the late 1800's. Today it is

Bluffs, Beaches, Lighthouses and Shipwrecks

a pretty area with benches to enjoy the shoreline, a picnic area with grills, and a very nice sandy swimming beach—might as well jump in right away for a swim! Anclam Park is designated as a kayak launch site. As you launch, keep an eye down for the shipwreck Emeline. She was a three masted schooner that capsized off Baileys Harbor in 1896 and was towed to this pier, she lies broken in about 18 feet of water—perhaps a bit deep as we were not able to locate her.

It's a beautiful sunny day and fairly calm in the harbor, as we glide off the jetty and head towards Baileys Harbor marina. Just north of Anclam Park is Harbor Fish Market and Grille, which has an outdoor seating area in summer, pull up the kayaks, relax, and eat with a view.

Then we head towards the Ridges Sanctuary Beach. Just before the sandy beach, our first lighthouse, the Front Baileys Harbor Range Light is located. The range light built in 1869 is a white tower square at the base, but midway up the corners are cut back to create an octagonal tower with a red light. 950 feet straight behind the Front Range Light is the Back Range Light which has a white light. Mariners were instructed to keep the white light directly above the red light as they entered the harbor for safe passage.

Kayak Wisconsin, Door County Peninsula

Someone must not have listened to the range light instructions as there is an unidentified shipwreck just off the range lights after the public harbor marina. She lies in about 15 feet of water and her centerboard and sides are visible.

Head northeast out of Baileys Harbor towards Toft's Point and the old Bailey Harbor "birdcage" lighthouse. This lighthouse was needed shortly after the town was formed due to the hazardous reefs on both sides of the harbor. It was built of cream colored brick from Door County and is one of only three lighthouses still equipped with the birdcage style of lantern. The lighthouse was used only for 14 years as it was too close inside the harbor and too many ships were running aground on the shoals. It was replaced by the Cana Island Lighthouse and the Front and Rear

Bluffs, Beaches, Lighthouses and Shipwrecks

Baileys Harbor Range Lights located at Ridges Sanctuary that we just passed. The lighthouse island with the old birdcage lantern light, is now private property, so please enjoy it from the water.

One of the ships that ran aground was the Christina Nilsson, a schooner with three masts built in Manitowoc Wisconsin. She was seeking shelter from a blizzard in Baileys Harbor in 1884 and ran aground. As you look up at the old Bailey Harbors birdcage lighthouse, take a little time to look down too, the Christina Nilsson is broken and scattered in only 15 feet of water under you just off the end of the island. As an added testament to why the old Baileys Harbor birdcage Lighthouse was not successful, there is another unidentified shipwreck just north off the island again in 15 feet of water.

As the shipwrecks can attest to, Tofts Point reef extends a very long way out into the lake, and we had a choice—face the white caps breaking on the rocky shoal, or head about a half mile out and around. We chose to meet the breakers head on and weave our way through the rocky reef. Tricky and thrilling as several whitecaps came up and over and inside our kayak skirts! Toft's Point is entirely a nature preserve. It consists of 743 acres of an old resort with cabins and a historic limestone circular kiln that are still intact. The shoreline is wave cut dolomite cliffs with trees that are old growth remnants and limestone cobble beaches. Landing and exploring would not have been easy on our paddling day, but on a calm day, this area looks like an incredible area to delve into.

'Round the point and head into tranquil Moonlight Bay—OK, OK, not quite tranquil today, but still a little more secluded from the winds. Must have been a great night when this bay was named—maybe we should stick around until dark to find out. . . There is a public primitive nature area on the north side of the bay called Bedrock Beach State Natural Area. It has no trails and the "beach" is literally the bedrock, but it is a quiet area for a break on the shoreline. Also, inside the bay, Reibolds Creek comes out of Mud Lake into Lake Michigan. Named Murphy Public Park, this is a quiet area to launch a kayak, but has no parking area. The beautiful Moonlight Bay has its own shipwreck, the Ebenezer, a two masted schooner built in Wisconsin stranded here in 1880. She lies broken and scattered in 14 feet of water, take some time to look for her but we did not find her.

On the northern tip of Moonlight Bay is Bues Point. There is a public boat landing here with one ramp and limited parking. This is our half

way point and a good spot to downsize this leg into two smaller paddles.

We head just a bit further past a tiny bay called Spike Horn (love to hear the story on how it got its name) to Cana Island and its famous lighthouse. It is a popular tourist attraction for good reason as it is a perfect example of a lighthouse, is over 140 years old, and although it is located on an island—in low water levels it is accessible by walking across the lake—oh, OK, by a natural causeway connected to the mainland. The Cana Island lighthouse initially was fueled by lard that needed to be carried up 97 spiral steps to reach the gallery light, wonder if the light keeper counted them every night? The round ball at the top of the tower is the vent that removed the smoke and soot. The 3rd order freznel lens is now powered by electricity and has a range of 18 miles. There have been many ship wrecks off the island (seven at one time in the Alpena Gale in 1880 and in 1928 the freighter M. J. Bartelme went aground in fog). Therefore, we are careful in our approach to land, especially since there are tourists up in the lighthouse tower watching…with cameras.

After a light picnic lunch on the island, exploring the lighthouse, exhibits, and the restrooms, we are in our boats again and pushing off the rocks on the

Bluffs, Beaches, Lighthouses and Shipwrecks

quieter side of the island. Here is your next chance at finding a shipwreck: there is an unidentified shipwreck scattered and broken north of the causeway to Cana Island, possibly a schooner.

Now the shoreline is public again with the Baileys Harbor Boreal Forest and Wetlands Nature Area. It is a rare, pristine forest of coniferous trees including the balsam fir, white spruce, white cedar and hemlock. The forest floor is covered by a dense mat of pine needles and organic matter that is prevented from decomposing by the cold temperatures. This type of forest is not usually located this far south. It is dotted with a 1 ½ mile alkaline rock shore—bedrock beach which hosts migratory shorebirds and waterfowl and is one of only a few known nesting areas for the goldeneye diving duck.

We round into North Bay and pass the Gordon Lodge. If you prefer restaurants to picnic lunches, the Gordon Lodge's Top Deck Restaurant in a beautiful remodeled boat house has a great garden patio and views of North Bay. There is easy landing on their private sand beach. Gordon Lodge is an upscale resort on the quiet side of Door County. Gravity Trails offers small group kayak tours including sunset tours, or for an

Kayak Wisconsin, Door County Peninsula

unusual workout—Stand Up Paddleboard (SUP) tours into North Bay from Gordon Lodge.

As you paddle your standard kayak or stand up paddleboard, stay towards the middle of North Bay as this bay is shallow. If you keep the southern point of North Bay directly behind you and the North Bay boat landing in front of you as you angle across the bay, then you will literally pass over another sunken shipwreck. The Cherubusco, a three masted schooner, built in Milwaukee, was stranded in November 1874 (yes one hundred and forty years ago!). She lies in about 10 feet of water about three fourth of the way across the bay and approximately half way into the bay. She is mostly intact but buried in the golden sand and only her center trunk and sides are visible. Seems like a treasure hunt when you find her, gave us goose bumps...

Then head to the north side of bay towards the big L shaped private dock and glide into their little cove. Here lies yet another sunken shipwreck. The Boaz, a three masted double centerboard schooner built in Sheboygan lies broken and buried in only about 10 feet of water. Her centerboard and side hulls are clearly visible protruding out of the bottom. It's a quiet area to swim, snorkel and search, but please no touching

Bluffs, Beaches, Lighthouses and Shipwrecks

or taking as it is actually illegal to salvage Wisconsin's historic shipwrecks.

After the excitement of the shipwrecks, it's back to the peaceful bay. On the left side of the bay is the North Bay State Natural Area. 'Really cool that so much of this paddle has included primitive natural areas ripe for exploring.

When you think you are running out of bay water, you are, and that's where you'll find the North Bay boat landing. It has an old concrete pier with a bench, perfect for relaxing and reminiscing about our day.

Perhaps there is time to chill out and gather at Bailey Harbor's Door County Brewing Company where the beer is inspired by the Door's landscape.

Logistics:

Directions to Anclam Park, Baileys Harbor:

45.0587, -87.1238. Located off Highway 57 on the southern end of Baileys Harbor, turn on Anclam Road into the parking lot. Free to launch!

Kayak Wisconsin, Door County Peninsula

Directions to Baileys Harbor Marina and boat launch:

45.0657, -87.1227. Highway 57 in downtown Baileys Harbor at the intersection of County F. Restrooms available, fee to launch.

Directions to Ridges Road kayak launch:

45.0674, -87.1223. Lakeview Road, Baileys Harbor. From Highway 57 in downtown Baileys Harbor, turn on Ridges Road and immediately turn right on dead-end Lakeview Road. Carry in access. We have not tried this launch site, Anclam Park or Ridges Sanctuary Park beach is easier. No fee.

Directions to Ridges Sanctuary Beach Park:

45.0695, -87.1180. 2301 Ridges Road, Baileys Harbor. From Highway 57 in downtown Baileys Harbor, turn on Ridges Road and drive .4 miles to the beach parking area. Restrooms, picnic area, no fees.

Bluffs, Beaches, Lighthouses and Shipwrecks

Directions to Moonlight Bay, Murphy Park, Reiboldt's Creek launch:

45.0957, -87.0819. Highway Q. From Highway 57 just north of Baileys Harbor, take County Q about 3 miles, launch is a gravel road on the right side of the road before you go over the bridge over Mud Creek before Moonlight Bay Drive.

Directions to Bues Point Landing:

45.0817, -87.0678. 8510 Bues Point Road. From Highway 57 just north of Baileys Harbor, take County Q about 3 miles to Cana Island Road, after about 1 mile when Cana Island Road turns sharply left—stay straight on Bues Point Road, when Bues Point Road turns sharply left, turn right to launch site. There is one concrete ramp with a dock, parking along the road, fee to launch.

Directions to North Bay Boat Launch:

45.1514,-87.0610. From Highway 42, just north of where Highway 57 meets 42 at Sister Bay, turn east on Highway ZZ, go about 2 ¼ miles and turn south on North Bay Road. Travel about 2 miles on North Bay Road and follow it as it turns into a gravel road down to the North Bay boat launch. Fee to launch.

Directions to Cana Island and Lighthouse:

45.0906, -87.0513. 8800 E. Cana Island Road. From Highway 57 north of Baileys Harbor, turn east on Highway Q and drive about 3.5 miles, turn right on Cana Island Road and follow the road until it ends. Parking is extremely limited (maybe it is best to just come by kayak!). Walk across the causeway and up to the lighthouse. Charge is $6-$10, depending on whether you wish to climb to the top of the lighthouse tower. Open from May to October daily 10am-5pm.

Location of shipwrecks:

Emeline: off Anclam Park in Baileys Harbor in about 18 feet of water. Sorry, we haven't found her, you are on your own, let us know if you find her!

Bluffs, Beaches, Lighthouses and Shipwrecks

Unidentified wreck: 45.0677, -87.1188. Just north of the Baileys Harbor boat launch and marina and just off the range lights in 10-15 feet of water.

Christina Nilsson: 45.0545, -87.0977. Baileys Harbor, just south off the old birdcage Harbor Light island in about 15 feet of water

Unidentified wreck: 45.0550,-87.0957. Baileys Harbor, just north off the old birdcage Harbor Light island in 10-15 feet of water.

Ebenezer: scattered and broken in Moonlight Bay inside of the quarry dock cribs. Sorry, we haven't found her, you are on your own, good luck!

Unidentified wreck: 45.0900, -87.0484. Cana Island- just north of causeway, possibly a schooner, broken and scattered in 10 feet of water.

Cherubusco: 45.1417, -87.0621. Middle north side of North Bay in about 10 feet of water.

Boaz: 45.1390, -87.0514. North Bay, near Marshall Point in a little cove by a private L shaped dock in 10 feet of water.

Kayak Wisconsin, Door County Peninsula

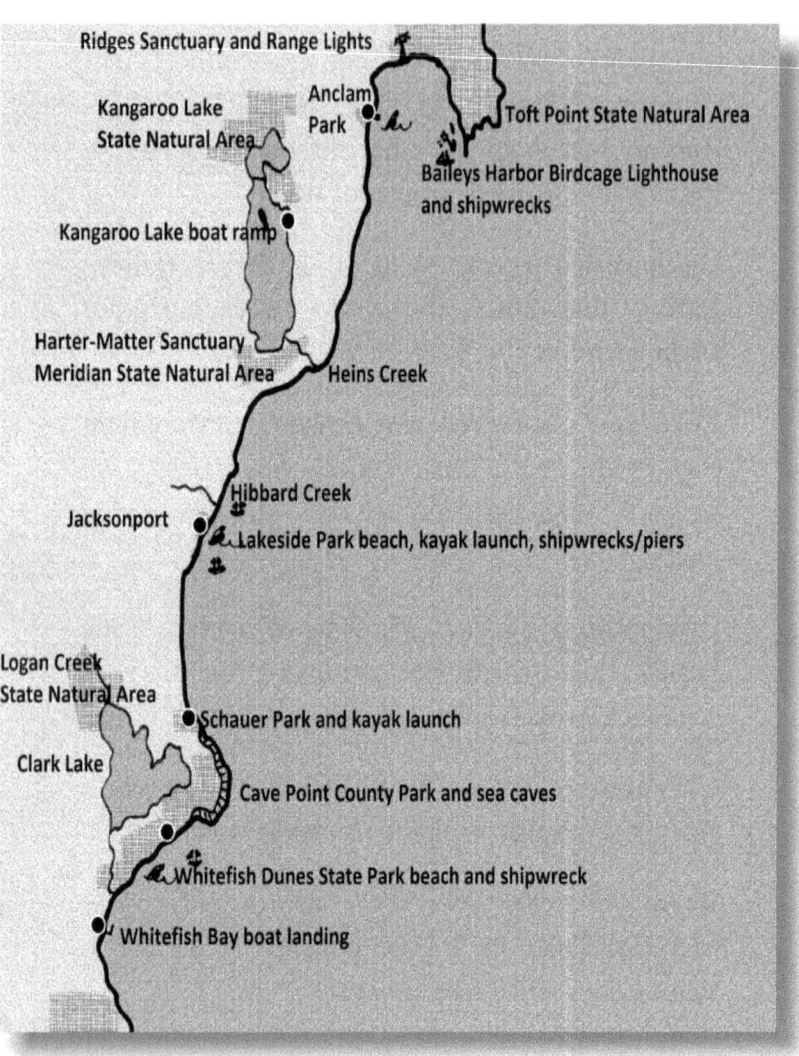

Bluffs, Beaches, Lighthouses and Shipwrecks

Leg 16

Cave Point

Baileys Harbor to Jacksonport to Whitefish Dunes State Park

With Cave Point's caves, sand dunes and beaches at Whitefish Bay, and lots of shipwrecks

10 miles

Whoosh! Boom! Cave Point's caves make some tremendous noise. Highlights on this leg include Bailey Harbor's Anclam Park with a great swimming beach, a mostly unperturbed shoreline from Baileys Harbor to the point off Kangaroo Lake, Jacksonport with its very nice swimming beach and shipwrecks very visible from kayaks, the spectacular caves at Cave Point, and the immense sand dunes and beaches of Whitefish Dunes State Park. A bit of everything in this gem of a paddle!

This paddle will be a bit longer if you paddle into the bay to Jacksonport, so you may want to cut it in half and paddle from Baileys Harbor to Lakeside Park in Jacksonport for a 6 mile paddle, and then from Jacksonport, past Cave Point to Whitefish Dunes State Park for another 6 mile paddle. I have enjoyed that shorter paddle with my son Matthew with shipwrecks and caves. If you are just looking for the excitement of Cave Point, then the most popular kayak launch is Schauer County Park and paddle southwest to Cave Point and return back to Schauer's boat landing for a 4 mile paddle—remember to choose a calm day. A little nervous to do this on your own? Never fear, Lakeshore Adventures in Bailey's Harbor offers Cave Point or shipwreck tours, try it out in a clear bottom kayak.

We have done Cave Point on other days when it was too windy and wild to get close to the caves so we waited patiently for the perfect day to do this paddle. A chilly late Autumn day in October offered a gentle 10 knot wind from the northwest, making the Lake Michigan side of the Peninsula the lee, quiet side and our perfect opportunity to investigate inside the caves at Cave Point. To use the little wind coming from the north, we put in at Anclam Park in Bailey's Harbor and paddled south to Cave Point and Whitefish Dunes State Park. Anclam Park is a great swimming beach and Baileys Harbor was calm and protected, but way too cold to swim in October. In fact, any time in fall for paddling Lake Michigan makes a drysuit or wetsuit mandatory apparel, and still swimming did not occur to us as we started out with the temp in the 30's.

Bluffs, Beaches, Lighthouses and Shipwrecks

Baileys Harbor was named after Captain Bailey who came into the harbor during a storm in 1848, liked what he saw and talked his boss into building the town for a limestone quarry and lumbering. The little peninsula of Anclam Park is the leftover of the old pier from back in Captain Bailey's days. If you look to the northern point of Bailey's Harbor you will see the old Bailey Harbor lighthouse that has a unique birdcage lantern at its top. It is located on a little private island and is no longer in use.

We rounded the gentle southern end of Baileys Harbor and enjoyed the basically pristine shoreline for several miles to the next point. Although this area is not designated parkland, there are few roads to the shoreline to interrupt the peaceful coastline. Björklunden, the northern campus of Lawrence University, has over a mile of untouched shoreline with meadows and woods. "Björklunden" is Swedish for "the birch grove by the lake". Door Shakespeare offers outdoor theatre in the Björklunden garden, so we all can discover this gem along the shore.

Kangaroo Lake is the largest inland lake in Door County and it lays less than a half mile from the Lake Michigan shoreline. That is because it was once part of Lake Michigan and as the glacial water receded the high dunes separating Kangaroo

Kayak Wisconsin, Door County Peninsula

Lake from Lake Michigan formed the lake. The name may be a corruption of a local Native American name, as we are pretty sure there are no wild kangaroo's hopping about in Door County's north woods. Some people feel that the lake looks like a kangaroo with the north end the head? Kayak Kangaroo Lake for the large amounts of wetlands that have deer, fox, coyotes, and quite a few species of birds to discover around the edge of the lake. The north end of the lake is designated non motorized vessels only and is mostly surrounded by undisturbed forested shoreline of fir and tamarack. It is home to the Kangaroo Lake State Natural Area and is only one of two known breeding areas for the Hines Emerald Dragonfly. The Wisconsin DNR recommends putting in at the east end of the Highway E causeway.

The larger south end of Kangaroo Lake is accessible by Kangaroo Lake Beach Road on the west and at the end of South Kangaroo Lake Drive on the east shore. At the south end of Kangaroo Lake there is the Harter-Matter Sanctuary and Meridian State Natural Area, with Heins Creek flowing out of this to Lake Michigan at the point as we paddle by. After Heins Creek, we pass the 45th parallel which is halfway between the equator and North Pole! Meridian

Bluffs, Beaches, Lighthouses and Shipwrecks

Park and State Natural Area is an inland park on Highway 57 with a wayside to announce this call to fame. Guess this explains why we are not sweating with palm trees, but also not in a perpetual winter either.

Two miles after Heins Creek we pass Hibbard Creek which is an important trout spawning location due to good water quality and it's generally cobblestone bottom. Most of its shoreline is forested. You may be passing historical ground as this might be the site of a siege by Ottawas on the Iroquois tribe. A Native American burial ground has been located in the nearby town of Jacksonport. Perry Hibbard started a lumbering business near this creek named after him.

It got a little rough in the bay by Jacksonport, so staying close to shore and stopping in Jacksonport, which is almost the perfect halfway point, would be a great idea. Jacksonport was a Potawatomi settlement before it became a busy logging and fishing village.

Lakeside Park in downtown Jacksonport, smack dab in the middle of the shallow bay, has a wonderful sand and rock beach, picnic areas with grills and the beloved restrooms. The park also boasts not one but three shipwrecks! It is here that the remains of three piers from Jacksonport's fishing heyday lay on the lakebed and the three doomed schooners lay alongside the remnants of the piers. The two masted schooner Perry Hannah was blown into one of the piers during the Great Alpena Blow in October 1880, the three-masted schooner Cecilia was dragged ashore anchors and all and into the pier in 1885, and not to be out done, the Annie Dall was driven ashore in 1898. Guess this Jacksonport Bay can get awfully rough in windy weather.

After a rest break and time to explore Jacksonport, head south along the shoreline for two miles to Schauer Park. Look for the white parking lot area and boat ramp at the northern end of the park. Other than that, Schauer Park is undeveloped and has almost a quarter mile of rocky shoreline to enjoy some seclusion.

The shoreline starts to grow with wave-worn limestone cliffs as we near Cave Point County Park at the next big point. Anytime after the houses end, you can pull up on the rocks and explore this truly fabulous park. Found a little cove to land and set up lunch by the bluffs for a fantastic view out to the lake, the other side of the point we came from and the spectacular cliffs, pools of water on the rocks and big canopy of pines above. Cave Point offers great strolling up

Bluffs, Beaches, Lighthouses and Shipwrecks

above along the cliff's edge with the fresh scent of the pines, or some fossil hunting on the exposed rocks. The cliffs are made up of a remnant of a prehistoric warm sea that once covered the area and there are sea shell and coral reef fossils to be discovered. This may "only" be a county park, but it is one of the best jewels on the Door Peninsula and not to be missed—by water and on top looking down.

We hopped back into our kayaks to explore the mile of caves, it was so calm that there was no whooshing and booming with huge crashing of waves that spray all the way up to the top of the

curved cliffs over 20 feet above. We were able to glide into the sea caves and enjoy the underwater caves and rock formations. The clear water really shows off the underwater rocks and the blue sky, teal water and white cliff walls are truly dramatic. Well worth our wait for a peaceful day.

As we round Cave Point we glide into Whitefish Bay. Stay alert as we head towards the beach, because one of the newest shipwrecks to be found is in Whitefish Bay just 700-800 feet off shore. The Australasia, a gigantic wooden schooner caught fire, burned to the waterline and sank in 1896 leaving a debris field the size of a football field, and yet it was found just a few years ago. Now it can be your turn to find it.

And just when you think the fun is over, Whitefish Dunes State Park begins with a mile of sandy beach flanked by the tallest sand dunes in the whole state of Wisconsin. Slide up on the shore by the north beach access.

Whitefish Dunes State Park beach has about a one mile sandy beach to stroll. Take the time to walk the shoreline and watch for diving ducks or find your own private beach area for tanning and swimming—oh well, perhaps not today. . .

Bluffs, Beaches, Lighthouses and Shipwrecks

Perchance a stretch of your legs after a day of kayaking would be a good idea. Whitefish Dunes State Park has 14.5 miles of hiking trails. Explore the forested sand dunes, wetlands with a boardwalk, hardwood forests with many exposed rocks, or Whitefish Creek. Climb the dunes up to "Old Baldy" the tallest of the mighty sand dunes on the western shore of Lake Michigan. Not high enough? Then climb the observation platform for even more incredible views of Whitefish Bay. The brachiopod trail gives a geological story of Whitefish Dunes and even has a fossil rock wall with brachiopod fossils that are common on the Door Peninsula. Not enough exercise for the day yet? Then you can continue hiking back to Cave Point and enjoy the swoosh of the waves creating caves from above!

Logistics:

Directions to Anclam Park Baileys Harbor— good park for kayak launching:

45.0587, -87.1238. Located off Highway 57 on the southern end of Baileys Harbor, turn on Anclam Road into the parking lot. No fee and there are restrooms!

Kayak Wisconsin, Door County Peninsula

Directions to Lakeside Park Jacksonport:

44.9786, -87.1830. 6211 Lake Park Drive. Located off Highway 57 downtown Jacksonport with a wonderful beach and picnic areas. No fees but there are restrooms!

Directions to Schauer Road Park boat ramp:

44.9454, -87.1852. 5648 Schauer Road. From Highway 57 south of Jacksonport, take North Cave Point Road south, then left on Schauer Road to north end of park. Nice gravel parking lot, no fees, no restroom.

Directions to Whitefish Dunes State Park:

44.9211, -87.1961. From Highway 57 north of Sturgeon Bay, take County Road WD (for Whitefish Dunes, road is also called Clark Lake Road) east approximately 3.8 miles, turn right into the state park entrance road. After the park entrance booth, park behind the booth to unload/load your kayaks and then park in the parking lots. It is a bit of a long carry in down the beach hill. The kayak launch is right before the beach (to avoid the crowds). Don't choose this take out spot on windy days as the riptides may be strong. State Park fee, great visitor center and restrooms!

Directions to Whitefish Bay Road boat launch:

44.9057, -87.2159. This is an alternative takeout spot two more miles south of our take out spot. From Highway 57, turn east onto Whitefish Bay Road (County T) and drive about 2 miles to the lake (keep straight when County T turns right). At the lake there is a parking lot and the kayak launch is to the left of the pier. Fee for launch, and we did not see any restrooms.

<u>Shipwreck and piers location:</u>

Piers with the Cecelia, Perry Hannah and Annie Dall near by: 44.9779,-87.1814 and 44.9795,-87.1808. Off of Jacksonport's Lakeside Park.

Australasia: 44.9211, -87.1867. Lies in 15 feet of water in Whitefish Bay, off of Whitefish Dunes State Park.

Kayak Wisconsin, Door County Peninsula

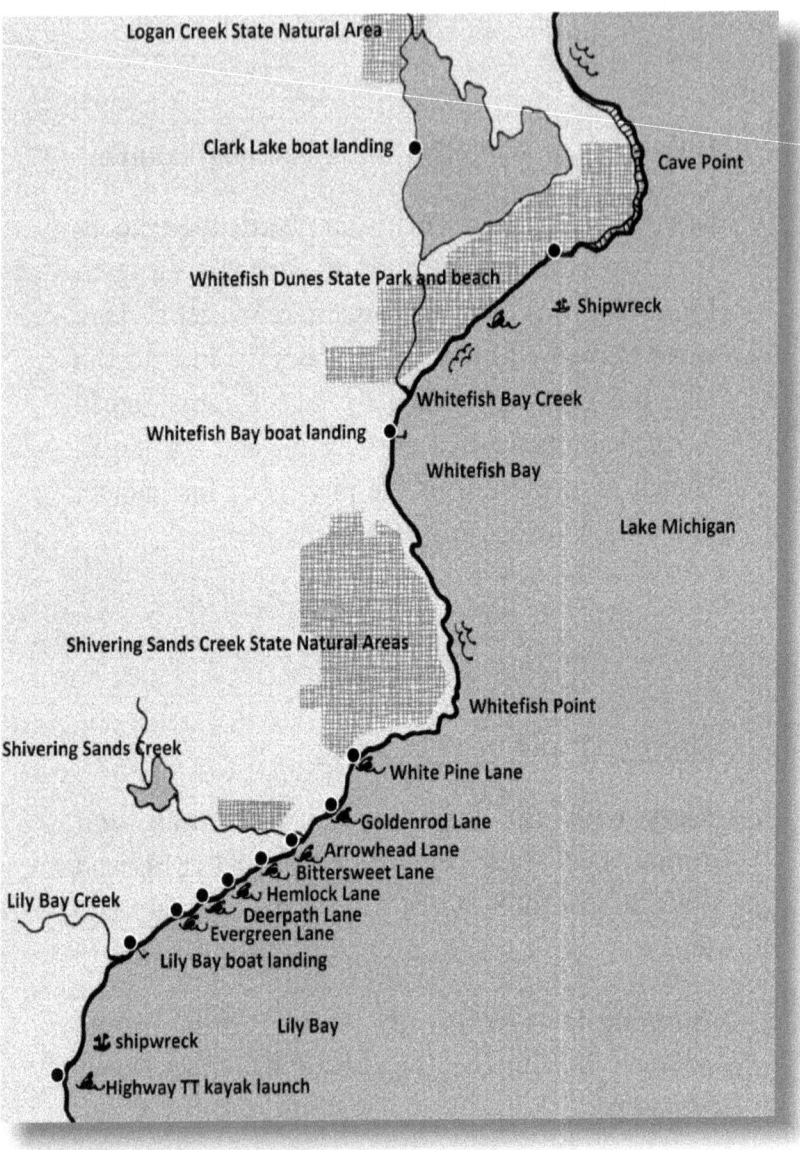

Leg 17

Dunes and Shipwrecks

Whitefish Bay to Lily Bay
With the tallest sand dunes this side of Lake Michigan, sandy beaches, and fun shipwrecks
10 miles

Paradise. The purpose of this paddle = perfect paradise. We were so pleased with this paddle, we brought our sister Becky back up the very next weekend to experience it. Sandy bay beaches after sandy bay beaches, the hugest sand dunes this side of Lake Michigan, and the excitement of a can't hardy miss it shipwreck and a newly found shipwreck.

'Recommend this paddle on a glorious summer day. We chose a steamy July day, and with the prevailing summer south winds, we put in at Lily Bay and paddled with the surf north to Whitefish Bay and Whitefish Dunes State Park. Part the paddle at about the halfway point at White Pine Lane, a public access with you guessed it, white pines and a little path to the bay with a great sand beach.

Kayak Wisconsin, Door County Peninsula

As always, check the marine weather forecast. For us there was a midrange wind (10-14 knots) so this was an intermediate paddle with 2 foot swells and the occasional 1 foot whitecaps. Put in at Lily Bay kayak launch and beach just north of Sturgeon Bay. There aren't any lily pads, just curved sand beach perfect for driftwood hunting and an early morning swim. Stop and appreciate the view—Lake Michigan's horizon, and hopefully light fluffy clouds are dancing above the sparkling water just as it was for us.

Head north and stick fairly close to the shoreline. Here is your surprise. After only about a half mile

Bluffs, Beaches, Lighthouses and Shipwrecks

you may notice some rocks sticking up or some whitecaps bopping unexpectantly just off shore. I chose to avoid the whitecaps while Rick headed straight to them for surfing. "Babs it's a ship". "No there aren't any shipwrecks in Lily Bay." "Get over here, I'm telling you it is a ship". "OK, OK. . .it is a ship!" Poor thing is not as famous as the Fleetwing, Meridian or Ocean Wave, but the City of Glasgow was once one of the "Big Four" largest ships sailing the Great Lakes. She began as a mighty wooden bulk steamer built in West Bay City Michigan in 1891. Sadly in 1907 she suffered a devastating fire and had to be cut from her original 295 feet in length to just 195 feet and converted to a barge. Her tragic end came in 1917 when her tow line parted and she was blown ashore in this beautiful bay. Since she has sat in her shallow grave for almost a century, her top half has sheared off and what we see today is just her substructure bones.

Shortly after leaving the can't miss it City of Glasgow shipwreck, the meandering Lily Bay Creek flows gently into the bay. Then the Lily Bay boat landing and dock sticks out into the bay like a thumb with its two bright orange diamond signposts calling you in.

After that comes a series of serene sand dune and beach stops: Evergreen, Deerpath, Hemlock and

Bittersweet Lanes. These aptly named lanes may only offer 50 feet of public access each but they pack a punch in those few feet. The gravel lanes are lined with wildflowers and trees canopy above leading to winding paths that ramble down over the classic sand dunes to sandy beaches. The sand dunes are covered in marram grass which has spider vein roots that hold the sand in place so that we can enjoy the warm sand beach. Bring your beach mat, spread it out, soak up some sunrays and enjoy a day at the beach.

Shimmering Sands Creek empties into the bay after Bittersweet Lane turning the bay a wee bit darker in color. Then more small trails wind

Bluffs, Beaches, Lighthouses and Shipwrecks

down the sand dunes from Arrowhead, Goldenrod and White Pine Lanes providing more picturesque opportunities to swim or picnic at our midpoint of our Lake Michigan paradise paddle. White Pine Lane is the approximate halfway point of our day paddle.

Behind the 20 to 30 foot high sand dune ridge is the Clay Banks State Natural fen area, Shivering Sands Unit. This is a natural wetland formed when ancient bays were closed off with sand dune deposits. The Shivering Sands fen is fed by numerous springs from the bedrock, and has three small lakes including Dunes Lake which Shivering Sands creek flows from. Pools and ponds saturate the forest with sedges, grasses, and mosses, surrounded by birches, spruce, cedar, beech, hemlock and white pines. The fen provides quiet areas for otters, hares, porcupines, mink and coyotes along with over 100 species of birds. The sand dunes are home to several threatened plants including dune goldenrod, thistle, lake iris, and reed grass. Want to learn? Sedges have edges, rushes are round, grasses are hollow, what have you found? (Hilton Pond Center, York, South Carolina)

Whitefish Point stretches lazily out into Lake Michigan, but off this point the Ocean Wave schooner floundered in 1869 while heavy with stone from Moonlight Bay. She lies broken on the lake bed but her bow is intact and has a rare screaming eagle figurehead. She is on the National Register of Historic Places but unfortunately lies deep in 110 feet of water, so no chance of seeing her from above the waterline. Did ya bring scuba gear?

Rounding Whitefish Point brings us into large Fisherman's Bay—oh wait that was in the 1800's, now it is called Whitefish Bay. The Clark brothers had a commercial fishing operation on Whitefish Bay in the 1840's and may have been the origin for the name of the bay. Whitefish Bay has great fishing still for lake sturgeon, walleye, trout, and of course whitefish.

Paddle into the belly of the bay and you'll see the Glidden Lodge Pier and their private beach, but if you would like to stop for a supper on their restaurant patio, by all means pull up on the side of their beach. The next big brown pier is the Whitefish Bay boat landing and beach. This could be a more protected kayak take out and easier carry out than using Whitefish Dunes State Park.

Travel along the inner bay beach with homes in front and the state park behind. Soon Whitefish Bay Creek trickles soothingly into the bay from

Bluffs, Beaches, Lighthouses and Shipwrecks

Clark Lake. Thousands of years ago Whitefish bay used to be Clark Bay until the sand accumulated so much it cut Clark Bay into Clark Lake, the dunes, and our "new" Whitefish Bay. Clark Lake would be a good kayaking excursion on a windy day when the lake seems too formidable. There is a public boat landing on the western shore, Logan Creek State Natural area at the north end, and on the south end Whitefish Dunes State Park has a third of a mile public access area.

After the creek, the public beach begins and "Old Baldy", looks down at you. At 93 feet above lake level, he is the tallest of the tallest sand dunes this side of Lake Michigan. Sculling along the dunescape, you'll discover a beach path leading up to the dunes ridge trail and to Old Baldy.

Amazingly the Door Peninsula with Green Bay and Lake Michigan has 275 recorded shipwrecks with a high percentage in the shallow waters of the surf zone. Whitefish Bay is suspected of having a plethora of shipwrecks: Grey Eagle, Hungarian, DA Volkenburg, James Garrett, Otter, Success, and the Harrison, most of which were schooners but without known shipwreck locations. However in 2005, two jet skiers found the remarkable Australasia shipwreck just 700 feet off shore in about 15 feet of water. The big steamer originally was the largest wooden vessel built on the Great Lakes. The Australasia was unfortunately carrying coal when she caught fire outside of Baileys Harbor in 1896. She was abandoned but the ship headed on all ablaze and only sunk when it finally struck bottom in Whitefish Bay. Wreckage is a strewn over a huge area so enjoy searching below the waterline. Who knows maybe you'll find another next big shipwreck! Did ya bring snorkel gear?

Dip your paddle along the sandy shoreline to the north end of the beach before the rocky cave point begins. This is our planned take out spot. As you disembark, check out the sand—put a magnet to it and magnetite will cling to it because the sand is glacier debris that was dumped into Lake Michigan.

Since Whitefish Dunes beach is the largest public sand beach on the Door Peninsula, don't miss the opportunity to walk the mile long beach. Body surf the waves. Build a sand sculpture. Do a sand angel. Play, play, play in this perfect paradise.

Bluffs, Beaches, Lighthouses and Shipwrecks

Logistics:

Directions to Lily Bay kayak launch and beach:

44.8351, -87.2750. Corner of Highway TT at lakeshore From Highway 42/57 north of Sturgeon Bay, turn east on Highway TT, go approximately dead end at the lakeshore. Short carry in, parking on road, no fee, no restrooms.

Directions to Lily Bay boat landing:

44.8498, -87.2628. From Highway 42/57 north of Sturgeon Bay, turn east on Highway T, go approximately 4 miles and when Highway T turns north–go straight to the boat ramp. Parking is available, no restrooms, fee for launching.

Directions to Beach Lanes off Glidden Drive (Highway T):

From Highway 42/57 north of Sturgeon Bay, turn east on Highway T, go approximately 4 miles and turn north on Highway T (Glidden Drive). The following beach lanes are off Glidden Drive. Parking on the lane, please do not block the driveways. No fees, no restrooms.

Kayak Wisconsin, Door County Peninsula

Evergreen Lane: 44.8531, -87.2559.

Deerpath Lane: 44.8543, -87.2521.

Hemlock Lane: 44.8565, -87.2467.

Bittersweet Lane: 44.8589, -87.2405.

Arrowhead Lane: 44.8613, -87.2346.

Goldenrod Lane: 44.8642, -87.2283.

White Pine Lane: 44.8687, -87.2239.

Directions to Whitefish Bay Boat Landing and beach:

44.9057, -87.2159. From Highway 57 north of Sturgeon Bay (past Institute) at Valmy, turn east on Highway T/Whitefish Bay Road. Go approx 2 ½ miles, when Highway T turns south, continue straight on Whitefish Bay Road to the boat ramp parking lot. This is a much easier and safer kayak launch or take out spot than Whitefish Dunes State Park. Parking and Port-a-potty available. Fee required to launch.

Bluffs, Beaches, Lighthouses and Shipwrecks

Directions to Whitefish Dunes State Park:

44.9211, -87.1961. From Highway 57, turn east on Highway WD (Clarks Lake Road), drive about 3 ¾ miles to the Whitefish Dunes State Park entrance. Park and unload kayaks behind the entrance booth, then move your vehicle to the parking lot. A fairly long kayak carry. Launch kayaks north of swimming beach. State Park fee, restrooms and changing rooms available.

Shipwreck locations:

City of Glasgow: 44.8386,-87.2709. Lies in 3 feet of water in Lily Bay off North Lake Michigan Drive between Highways TT and T.

Australasia: 44.9211, -87.1867. Lies in 15 feet of water in Whitefish Bay, off of Whitefish Dunes State Park.

Kayak Wisconsin, Door County Peninsula

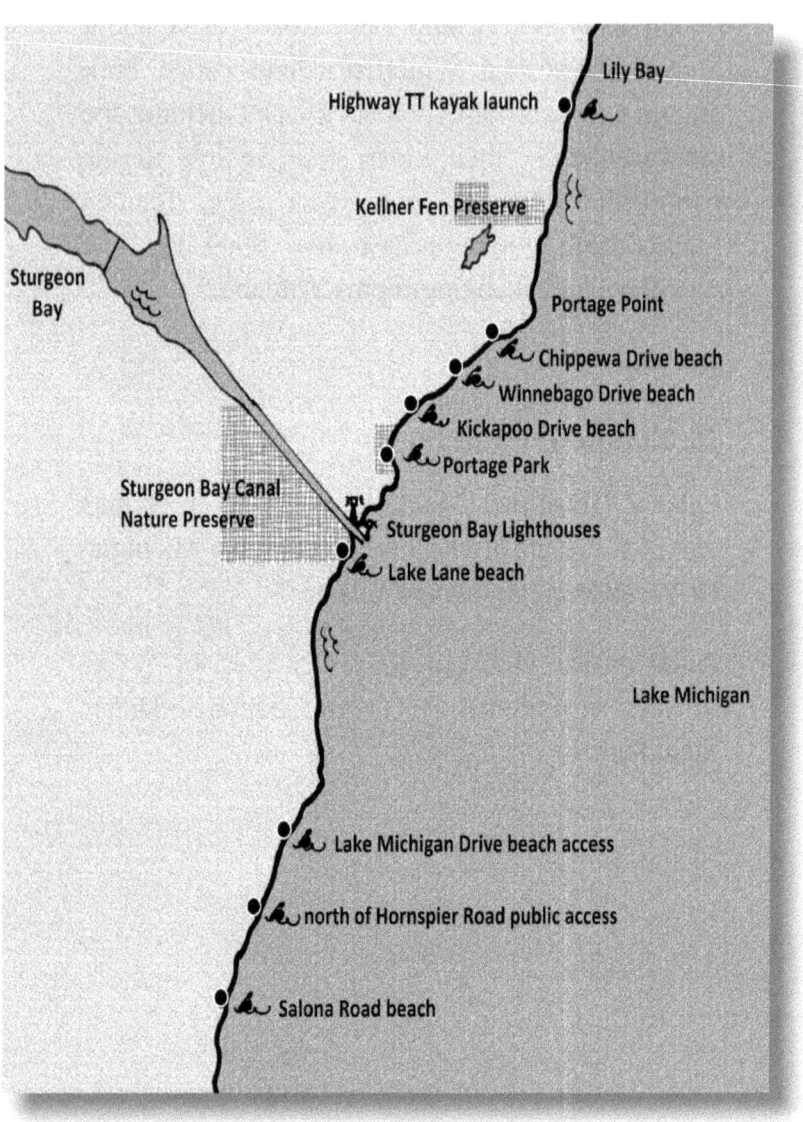

Leg 18

Beaches

Lily Bay, Portage Bay and Salona Road Beaches
*With Portage Park, Lake Lane, and Lake Michigan Drive beaches,
and the Sturgeon Bay Lighthouses*
6 miles

Beach baby, beach. . .this paddle may be only 6 miles long, but you can make it a whole day affair with some of the greatest beaches ever—why would you want a longer paddle?! Do this paddle on a toasty warm mid-summer day and bring your beach blanket and sunscreen lotion. And take time to enjoy the historic Portage Park and the lighthouses at the Sturgeon Bay channel.

This paddle includes our PPP: pristine personal paradise. So much so, we shared the beaches and lighthouses again with my son Matthew. So if you desire to spend more time at all the incredible beaches, then please divide this paddle and the Lake Lane Beach on the south side of Sturgeon Bay is the best half way point.

Launch at Lily Bay where County road TT turns at the lake. There is a path to carry your kayaks around the guard rail and then down to the sandy beach. Lily Bay is a longggg, six mile sand bay but only dips into the peninsula about one mile. Both points north and south are sandy bars, and there are an abundance of incredible sandy beach lanes for public access dotting the bay. County Road TT is the southernmost beach lane on lovely Lily Bay. Here is your first opportunity for a swim—why not start this day with a dip? That is what this day is all about.

Paddle south along the sandy coastline past several small meandering streams bubbling out to Lake Michigan. The streams flow from the Kellner Fen Preserve behind the shoreline homes. This area was part of post glacial Lake Nippising and now is cut off from present Lake Michigan by the high red clay bank and sand dune ridges. The Kellner Fen is a hidden area with fragile sedge mats floating on the old lake. The fen used to sport a small cranberry farm and also a frog farm for frog legs for restaurants. Now it is home to rare insects, birds and plants including two carnivorous plants. The deceptionally pretty Sundew firework looking plant has dew on its tentacles–except it isn't dew, it's a gel substance that insects stick to and then they slowly get eaten. The Pitcher Plant has deeply folded leaves, the pitcher, with a sweet smelling juice inside that lures insects in, and then they can't climb back out and slowly dissolve in the toxic chemical juice. Now this fen sounds like an interesting place to explore!

We stay safely in our kayaks and slip around Portage Point and sail on into Portage Bay. Now Portage Bay may only be two miles long and barely laps inland, but it is one of the most picturesque coves on the Lake Michigan side, and that is saying a lot. There are three public access lane beaches coming off of Lake Forest Park Road. Chippewa Drive beach lane is about a half mile as you enter the shallow Portage Bay, followed a half mile later by Buffalo Ridge Trail road which turns into Winnebago Drive beach lane, and not to be out done the Kickapoo Drive beach lane is another half mile into the bay. WOW, swim all day at each one and pick your fav.

We aren't done yet. One more half mile brings you to Portage Park and let your jaw drop. Here is the drop dead gorgeous beach—our PPP: pristine personal paradise. Keep it a secret and it'll be yours too. Slide up to the shore in front of the line of big boulders that help define Portage Park. 'Time to lay out once again the beach blanket and revel in the sun, sand, and surf under our paradise palm trees, err, pine trees. Bring out a Frisbee and play in the waves. Take time to explore this paradise, this history producing spot where the Native Americans portaged and carried their canoes all the way to Sturgeon Bay. You try carrying your canoe or kayak that one and a half mile carry and you'll realize the significance of the Sturgeon Bay shipping canal!

Reapply your sun screen and skim out over the surface of Lake Michigan. It only gets better as you paddle out into the mini bay. Turn south around the little point and be astounded by the not one, but three historic Sturgeon Bay lighthouses— the overlooked little green and white striped south pier head light, the bold red north pier head light and the vivid white lighthouse with the red roof on shore. Three for the price of one glance! Slip through the pier opening under the walkway to the historic bright red range light built in 1872 as a harbor light.

For a great view of the Sturgeon Bay shipping canal lighthouse, land on the Coast Guard station beach next to the north jetty. The lantern started as just the tower with the curved window light above, but it vibrated so much, they needed to add the support beams to steady it which gives it its unique appearance today. Originally, this lighthouse was brown, but painted the bright white to make it easier to see. This lighthouse with its 3rd order Frenzel lens can be seen for 18 miles away. You can walk to the lighthouse and out on the pier for a closer look at the range lights. The canal and the red wooden north pier head light was completed in 1882 with a fixed 6th order red Fresnel light.

In 1886 a lifesaving station was added on the property. Probably a good thing as the Pierpont, a two masted schooner stranded near this north pier in 1881 and only her stern section lies broken along the shore. This coast guard station is a very active station with up to 200 cases of sea and ice rescues a year...please don't be one of them. It is also a National Homeland Security station—so behave yourself (I tend to find that a little hard). Although it is a pretty beach, please do not swim here as it is not a designated swimming beach and probably not safe with the parade of boats heading up and down the channel.

Paddle across the shipping canal very carefully, especially in summer. This is a very busy channel, supposedly because no one wants to circumnavigate the entire Door Peninsula every day—really? It's just 200 plus miles around the peninsula, not to mention having to go through "Deaths Door" at the tip. Guess you could call the canal a little bit of a shortcut to Green Bay. Technically, the northern half of the Door

Peninsula is really now an island, maybe we should change its name to Door Island.

Head through the opening of the south jetty with the green and white range light and maybe a gull squawking on top and arrive at our next beach, Lake Lane Beach at the Sturgeon Bay Ship Canal Nature Preserve established in 2011. This is the largest public beach area along our shoreline today with its beautiful white sand beach surrounded by rolling sand dunes, ancient shorelines ridges called swale formations with towering white pines, hemlocks and maple trees. The preserve is home to bald eagles and osprey and is a resting spot for migrating birds. You could make this day a "beach and feet" day by hiking the trails at the preserve and then strolling the south pier for an outstanding view of all the lighthouses. The beach is a quiet spot with room to spread out the beach blanket and drink in the view of Lake Michigan's glittering horizon.

Take your time, this is a day not made for rushing. When you've lounged enough, glide back out on the lake south along the sandy shoreline of this gentle bay and past Rocky Point. After you have gone about two miles from the Sturgeon Bay channel there is about a half mile section of shoreline without homes called Clay Banks beach with access points off of Lake Michigan Drive

Kayak Wisconsin, Door County Peninsula

just north of Hornspier Road. Look for the thin sand trails leading to the water's edge. The Clay Banks beach accesses are hard to pick out without a GPS to guide you from the water, but that alone makes them worthwhile spots to find and enjoy!

Hornspier Road is a historic pioneer village area that turned to a ghost town by the 1920's. Around the Civil War years, W.H. Horn built, aw—you guessed it, a pier, but it was a very long thousand foot pier to avoid the shallow reefs, and underwater rock ledge. The town was a bustling lumber town with even a dance hall, but the dock and warehouse burned in 1871. Now all that is left is a small clearing in the woods near the lake. Go on a shipwreck quest as the Sea Bird schooner sprung a leak and her cargo grain swelled so much it burst the deck and hull at Horns Pier, but she and the pier location have never been found.

Clay Banks Creek runs south of Hornspier Road. The clear water creek with a sandy bottom produces brook stickleback that bass and northern pike like to feed on.

Shortly after, comes our favorite beach take out spot. At the end of Salona Road is a little beach access point in another gentle curved shoreline. Salona was another old town, but besides the fact

it had a post office, not much else is known. Why would they leave? Even on a hot summer day, we were the only ones on the whole beach for most of our lunch and swim. Add a few palm trees and you have a Jamaican paradise. This just might be our retirement home location—it is that awesome. Relaxed on our beach blanket, swam, wiggled our toes in the sand, and enjoyed the brilliant end of our sun filled day at the beaches.

Kayak Wisconsin, Door County Peninsula

Logistics:

Directions to Lily Bay kayak launch and beach:

44.8351, -87.2750. North of Sturgeon Bay, turn east on Highway TT and follow it to the lake where the road ends at a guard rail. There is a small path around the guard rail to carry kayaks to the beach.

Directions to the Beach Lanes off of Lake Forest Park Road (County Road TT):

From Highway 42/57 north of Sturgeon Bay, turn east on Highway TT, go approximately 4 miles and turn south before Lake Michigan where Highway TT continues south and is also called Lake Forest Park Road. The following beach lanes are off Lake Forest Park Road. Parking on the lane, please do not block driveways. No fees, no restrooms:

Chippewa Drive: 44.8126, -87.2895.

Winnebago Drive (continuation of Buffalo Ridge Trail): 44.8095, -87.2956.

Kickapoo Drive: 44.8056, -87.3034.

Bluffs, Beaches, Lighthouses and Shipwrecks

Directions to Portage Park:

44.8015, -87.3075. North of Sturgeon Bay after the Bayview (Highway 42/57) Bridge take the first intersection right (east) onto Utah St, then turn right on Cove Road, then take the first left onto Canal Road (Highway TT) travel about 2 ¼ miles and turn north on Lake Forest Park Drive then take the first right/east on Portage Park Drive (a little gravel road with a sign that says "no camping", we did not see an actual road sign or a park sign), when the gravel road curves left there are big boulders that define the carry in access to the kayak launch and beach.

Directions to the Coast Guard Station and Sturgeon Bay Lighthouse and North Pier head Lighthouse:

44.7944, -87.3127. 2501 Canal Road. North of Sturgeon Bay after the Bayview (Highway 42/57) Bridge turn right (east) onto Utah St, then turn right on Cove Road, then take the first left onto Canal Road (Highway TT) and follow it to the Coast Guard Station and the parking lot. Carry your boat to the beach inside the pier head. No fee, but no public restrooms either.

Kayak Wisconsin, Door County Peninsula

Directions to Lake Lane Beach and Sturgeon Bay Nature Preserve:

44.7916, -87.3150. 5200 Lake Lane, Sturgeon Bay. From Highway 42/57, take the last intersection south of crossing Sturgeon Bay over the Bayview Bridge in Sturgeon Bay south on County Road U/ Clay Banks Road, go about 1 ¾ miles and turn east on Lake Lane. Travel about 2 miles to the end of Lake Lane to the little parking lot at the end of Lake Lane. No fee!

Directions to Clay Banks beach access off Lake Michigan Drive:

44.7622, -87.3254. From Highway 42/57, take the last intersection south of crossing Sturgeon Bay over the Bayview Bridge in Sturgeon Bay south on County Road U/ Clay Banks Road, travel almost 4 miles south and turn east on Hornspier Road towards Lake Michigan. Drive about 1 ¼ miles to the end of Hornspier Road and turn north on Lake Michigan Drive. There is only off street parking and no sign designating the kayak launch and beach access. No fee or restrooms.

Bluffs, Beaches, Lighthouses and Shipwrecks

Directions to Clay Banks beach access off Lake Michigan Drive just north of Hornpier Road:

44.7559, -87.3308. From Highway 42/57, take the last intersection south of crossing Sturgeon Bay over the Bayview Bridge in Sturgeon Bay south on County Road U/ Clay Banks Road, travel almost 4 miles south and turn east on Hornspier Road towards Lake Michigan. Drive about 1 ¼ miles to the end of Hornspier Road and turn north on Lake Michigan Drive. Drive about 300 feet to the first street parking, no sign designating the kayak launch and beach access. No fee or restrooms.

Directions to Salona Road public beach access:

44.7481, -87.3357. From Highway 42/57, take the last intersection south of crossing Sturgeon Bay over the Bayview Bridge in Sturgeon Bay, go south on County Road U/Clay Banks Road. Drive about 5 miles south and then turn east on Salona Road towards Lake Michigan. Travel less than 1 mile to the end of the road. There is only off street parking. No fee, no restrooms.

Kayak Wisconsin, Door County Peninsula

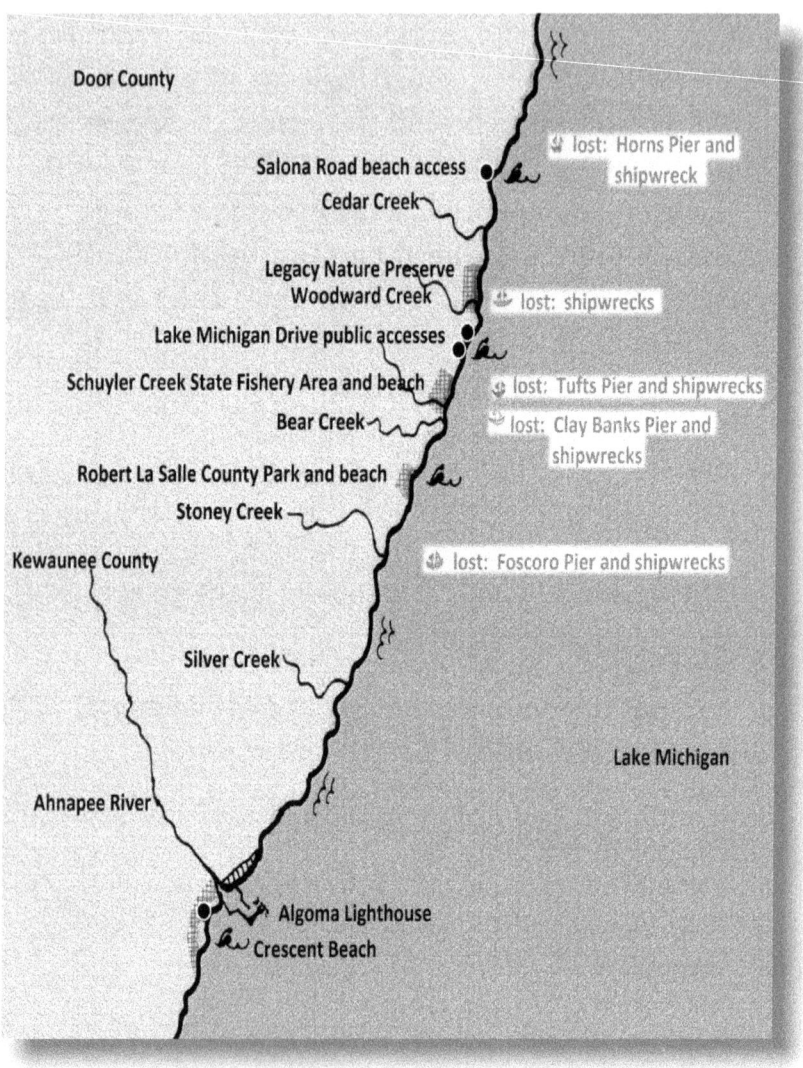

High Banks

Salona Road Beach to Algoma
With lost ghost towns, lost shipwrecks, and a beautiful tri-level shoreline
11.5 miles

"High Banks" is the nautical term the schooner sailors used to describe this undeveloped three tiered shoreline. The top tier of deep forest green woodlands is separated from the middle level of grassy upland by steep sandy banks jutting down to the pebble and boulder strewn beaches flowing out into Lake Michigan with its hidden rock shelves, sunken boulders. . .and hidden lost sunken ships.

Lost: Lost ghost towns, lost ships. The unlucky 13 lost ships: LaPetite, Glenham, S.L. Noble, Granville, Ida Bloom, F.A Fitch, Ottawa, John Everson, Granite State, Sea Star, Roving Star, Sea Bird and the Reciprocity all are waiting for us to discover them. Come join this ghost tour and help the Wisconsin Underwater Archeology Association discover the ghost towns, piers, and shipwrecks.

Kayak Wisconsin, Door County Peninsula

If this ghost tour appeals to you, you may want to divide the paddle into two day trips using La Salle County Park as your center launch spot.

We drive up to Salona Road, get out, load up the kayaks and just stop. Stop and gaze around. Love this beach, perhaps we should just throw down the beach blanket and loaf around all day.

Let your gaze drift north. Imagine a thousand foot pier jutting out into Lake Michigan. Visualize large three masted schooners moored at the end of the dock with their tall rigging. Notice the hustle and bustle as sailors unload the supplies from "down south" and load up the lumber, cedar posts, railroad ties and telegraph poles. Follow the line of the pier to the busy pioneer village on shore with fifteen buildings including warehouses, a post office, and a dance hall. During the Civil War W. H. Horn built this pier, it was destroyed in the October 1871 by the Chicago and Peshtigo fire that jumped over to Door County. The pier was rebuilt, but by the turn of the century as the lumber faded, so did Horns Pier—fading into a lost ghost town with no trace. The Sea Bird Schooner sprung a leak by Horn's Pier and its wheat grain swelled so much it broke apart and sank. She's our first shipwreck to search for. . .let's get kayaking!

Bluffs, Beaches, Lighthouses and Shipwrecks

We head south, and almost immediately the terrain switches from sandy beach to pebble beach and the banks begin to grow. Pass by Cedar Creek which is a possible old pier location, look for it, look for it.

Kreuter Legacy Preserve, a newer Door County Land Trust offers a beautiful stopping spot to explore this High Bank region. The high banks are actually the remnants of the long ago glacial shoreline beach, now raised high above the water. At the Legacy Preserve, you'll see the windswept high clay and sandy bank covered with dense forest of cedars, maple, and basswood with fields of milkweed and goldenrod below and on the high bank a bench perches overlooking the view of the lake. . .and us! There is 3000 feet of the public sandy and rocky shoreline with Woodward Creek rambling over the rocks into Lake Michigan. The Glenham schooner floundered ashore in 1872 and the crewmen were saved by a local man who lived near Woodward Creek. The LaPetite schooner capsized near here in 1903 and broke apart with debris washing up on this beach by the mouth of Woodward Creek, look for it, look for it.

Now Lake Michigan Drive follows the undeveloped shoreline and there are two public accesses off the road to launch kayaks or just for another rest way. Soon you will see Schuyler

Creek and the State Fishery area with about a thousand feet of shoreline that is yours to explore and swim as this is also known as Clay Banks Beach #1. The mouth of Schuyler Creek was the location of Tufts Pier which was a very active shipping port in the lumber years. Divers in the 1960's discovered two wrecks and an anchor off the mouth of creek, but no one ever returned to investigate and provide the locations of the shipwrecks, so now they have been lost twice. It is thought that two shipwrecks were the S.L. Noble and the Ida Bloom, both flat bottomed rectangle scows perfect for these shallow reefs. But unfortunately, the S. L. Noble schooner was pounded to pieces in a gale in 1868 while the Ida Bloom drifted ashore in 1879 and broke apart. Also the Granite State steam barge became stranded by the creek in a fall snowstorm in 1881. We looked for it, looked for it. . .

Just south of Tufts Pier was the town of Clay Banks with its own HUGE 1600 foot long pier located at Bear Creek. Now Bear Creek is a nice bubbling stream which supports wonderful native brook trout. But back in the pioneer days, on the banks of Bear Creek, Clay Banks was a thriving village, with a huge sawmill to go with the huge pier, three schools, a telegraph station and a post office. It too has its share of ghost shipwrecks.

The Sea Star in 1886 got caught in a storm and smashed into the Pier and sank just 180 feet away, and the Roving Star was at the dock when huge waves crashed into her causing her to hit bottom and break in half in 1892. Both of the star ships have never been found. We didn't find it, didn't find it...

Paddle up to La Salle County Park which show cases the High Banks area, the 440 foot pebble and boulder beach, a wildflower covered bank, grassy parkland, and another bluff topped with the frosting of rich forest. A small stream cuts through a sandy ravine on the southern edge of the park. We stopped for a picnic here and to enjoy the scenic views. It is a beautiful warm summer day, and we topped off our rest break with a delightful swim. This beach is also known as Braunsdorf Beach. Robert de La Salle, a French explorer, landed on this bank in 1679 and received supplies from the local Potawatomi people during his expedition of the Great Lakes. We are paddling in La Salle's footsteps, err wake, we in kayaks, La Salle and his party in canoes.

We are mighty explorers, so back in our kayaks we go. We head to Foscoro Point. OK, it's not really named that, but since it has no name, we can call the little point anything we want! We could have called it "U" point, as it is kind of where County Highway U curves to the shoreline, but Foscoro Point sounds better, and we are nearing the area of the pioneer lumber town of Foscoro by the banks of the Stoney Creek. Stoney Creek was dammed to help the logging operations with a large sawmill built across the stream. Foscoro was founded by three men: Foster, Coe and Rowe = Foscoro (probably better than Fostercoerowe). This was a true town with a telegraph station, post office, a general store, another thousand foot long pier, and of course the legendary shipwrecks. The Reciprocity schooner came ashore in 1880 in a big storm and is believed to have broken up near the Stoney Creek Reef. A tug belonging to Captain Fellows broke her mooring in 1893, and the John Everson tug capsized in 1895 and both sank off Stoney Creek. And the most famous, the Ottawa schooner went aground off shore on Foscoro Reef in 1911 with several crewmen dying attempting to reach shore. All these shipwrecks are just waiting for us to find them. Look for it, look for it. . .new tactic, since it is a hot summer day, we hopped into the water off Stoney Creek and swam for a while, "wait I think I'm standing on a shipwreck, oh, nope, just a boulder. . .wait here's one, oh, nope just another boulder, another boulder. . ."

Giving up, we hop back into our kayaks nice and cooled, and on with our exploring. We are now cruising into Kewaunee County, Potawatomi for "river of the lost" or "we are lost", but we are not lost—it's a beautiful day for sailing and paddling. Silver Creek is spring fed and is known for runs of trout and salmon as it dapples down to Lake Michigan shoreline. It is here that we can begin to see the hazy Algoma Lighthouse beckoning us several miles away.

Algoma was initially named An-Ne-Pe, "land of the great gray wolf", by the Potawatomi Native Americans, and the English and Irish pioneers called the town Ahnapee. A few years later, the city was renamed Algoma, another Native

Kayak Wisconsin, Door County Peninsula

American word meaning "park of flowers". In 1875 work was begun on the artificial harbor, and in 1893 when the 5th order Fresnel lens arrived, the pier light was finally lit. The original lighthouse was white and square. We paddle up close to the current red steel cylindrical pier head light that was part of a 1932 improvement project and now stands 42 feet high with red glass giving the north pier head lighthouse the signature red light that makes it a Great Lakes icon. The 1932 improvement project also included updating the harbor piers with design assistance by General Douglas MacArthur, an engineer at the time.

Bluffs, Beaches, Lighthouses and Shipwrecks

The north pier is 1102 feet long–giving us a great idea of how long the Foscoro, Tufts and Horn's Piers were. The south pier is 1530 feet long, demonstrating the length of the Clay Banks pioneer dock.

Inside the harbor at the end of the parking lot for the boat launch, is a little park area called Christmas Tree Point. At the end of every shipping season in the 1800's, over 50 schooners took one more sail, transporting Christmas trees to Milwaukee and Chicago. Folks would come to watch the Christmas tree schooners sail on south at this point. Up the river, the Lady Ellen, a two masted schooner scow that was built in town, was abandoned in the river and can at times be seen protruding from the water.

We cross the harbor entrance and followed the south pier with its myriad of fisherman on the pier. Algoma is the Midwest's salmon and trout capital which is keeping with its commercial fishing history. Glide up to Crescent Beach, yup, it does form a crescent and is half a mile long sandy beach with a boardwalk. We pull up close to the breakwater as it is closest to the parking lot. We share the beach with herring gulls, and an occasional dabbling duck teal and diving grebe.

Kayak Wisconsin, Door County Peninsula

OK, OK, we'll admit it, we aren't great explorers and treasure hunters of lost ghost town, piers and shipwrecks. We never found them, never found them...

Tag, you're it, your turn to "turn" famous shipwreck hunter and locate the lost ships and ghost towns. Happy paddling!

Logistics:

Directions to Salona Road public beach access:

44.7481, -87.3357. From Highway 42/57, take the last intersection south of crossing Sturgeon Bay over the Bayview Bridge in Sturgeon Bay, go south on County Road U/Clay Banks Road. Drive about 5 miles south and then turn east on Salona Road towards Lake Michigan. Travel less than 1 mile to the end of the road. There is only off street parking. No fee, no restrooms.

Directions to the Kreuter Legacy Door County Land Trust Preserve:

44.7288, -87.3405. No kayak launch–it would be a long carry and there is that natural high bank to climb down, but this is an awesome spot to stop while kayaking, or for hiking the 1+ miles of trails and scenic views. From Highway 42/57, take the last intersection south of crossing Sturgeon Bay over the Bayview Bridge in Sturgeon Bay, go south on County U/Clay Banks Road. Drive 5 miles south and turn east on Salona Road towards Lake Michigan. Turn south on Lake Michigan Drive 1.4 miles to the preserve parking area.

Directions to Beach kayak launch accesses off South Lake Michigan Drive:

44.7146, -87.3468 and 44.7124, -87.3478. Where South Lake Michigan Drive hugs the undeveloped shoreline, there are several kayak launches. From Highway 42 turn east on County Road J at Forestville about 5 miles. Turn north on County Road U and drive less than 1 mile and turn north on South Lake Michigan Drive and travel about a half mile to one mile for these launches. Roadside parking or pull off parking, carry down the bank to access the beach. No fee, no restrooms.

Kayak Wisconsin, Door County Peninsula

Directions to Schuyler Creek State Fishery Area:

44.7108, -87.3506. This is not designated as a kayak launch but would be a great rest break area while kayaking. From Highway 42 turn east on County Road J at Forestville about 5 miles. Turn north on county Road U and drive less than 1 mile and turn north on South Lake Michigan Drive. Travel about 400 feet to the parking area.

Directions to La Salle County Park:

44.6910, -87.3622. From Highway 42 turn east on County Road J at Forestville about 5 miles. Turn north on county Road U and drive about a half mile to Lower La Salle Road to access the parking lot closest to the beach. Drive to the end of the road to the parking lot. Short carry down steps to the beach. No fee, nice restrooms!

Directions to Crescent Beach in Algoma:

44.6063, -87.4357. OK, this one is easy. Crescent Beach is a half mile of sandy beach right on Highway 42 in downtown Algoma. The parking lot is at the north end of the beach next to the harbor. Restrooms are at end of Lake Street at the corner of Lake and Navarino Streets.

Kayak Wisconsin, Door County Peninsula

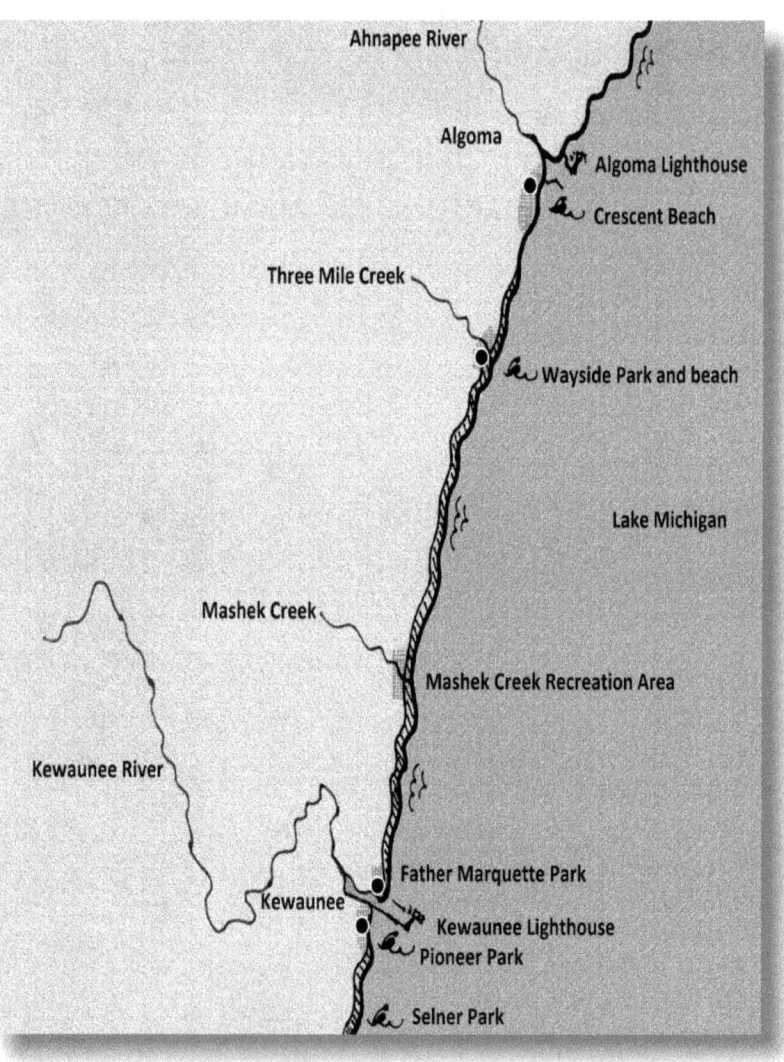

Leg 20

Sandy Bluffs

Algoma to Kewaunee
With scenic sandy bluffs, iconic Algoma and Kewaunee Lighthouses and two beautiful creeks
12 miles

Legendary last leg! A picturesque paddle with the towering sand bluffs, crystal clear pristine turquoise water, with the rocky lake bed twinkling beneath the waves. Which way to look? Up at the bluffs? Or down into the water? Either way is a delight! Add the two iconic lighthouses in Algoma and Kewaunee along with the two beautiful babbling brooks—Mashek Creek and Three Mile Creek and this is a paddle worth doing again and again. Picture perfect paddling.

A wee bit on the long side of our "approximately 10 mile" paddles, you could shorten this paddle at Wayside Park, 3 miles south of Algoma, but it would be a bit of a climb down to the shoreline on a narrow path.

It was a beautiful fall breezy day with the wind from the southeast. So we chose to paddle up the coast from Kewaunee to Algoma with some awesome gentle surfing. Kewaunee is a historic town, originally a large village of Potawatomi

Kayak Wisconsin, Door County Peninsula

Native Americans in the 1600's that was visited first by the explorer Jean Nicolet in 1634, followed by Father Marquette, and Robert de LaSalle in the 1670's. It grew up to be a lumber town, and now is the spirit of the lakeshore and the heart of Wisconsin's Schooner Coast. We put in at the Kewaunee Marina which does offer a kayak launch, along with a campground and showers, perhaps La Salle camped right here!

As we paddle under the Highway 42 bridge, on the right south bank is Harbor Park popular for shore fishing, with a gazebo and boardwalk. The small but mighty Tug Ludington docks here all summer. She was built for World War II and had fifty caliber machine guns mounted above her pilot house. The tug participated in the D Day invasion of Normandy, towing ammunition barges across the English Channel. In 1947, the tug came to Kewaunee to assist with harbor maintenance. Give her a thankful salute for her service as you pass her by.

On the left north bank is Harbor Point Park, a quiet peaceful green grass point with a boardwalk along the large fishing pier built over old wood moorings. It is here that the ferry, Badger, docked when it first started car ferry service across Lake Michigan in 1892. At the end of the small breakwater in the harbor, we could turn north to

Bluffs, Beaches, Lighthouses and Shipwrecks

Father Marquette Park memorializing his visit to Kewaunee and beach for launching kayaks well protected by wave action from the breakwater walls.

We chose to head towards the end of the harbor to check out the Kewaunee Lighthouse. In the 1850's a pair of piers were built and by 1891, for the safety of the schooners, pier range lights were established at the end of the piers with a fog horn house added to the south pier range light in 1909. In 1930, the south range light was destroyed when a railroad ferry hit the pier, so a light tower was built atop the fog house. This is what we see today, with the first story covered in white metal plates to support the weight of the tower and lantern room, while the second story is white shingles capped with its bright red roof. The octagonal lantern room sits on a four sided tower topped with a cast iron railing and still shines with a fifth order Fresnel lens. The poor north pier just has a sad overlooked little red and white striped light.

If you would go around the south point and the Kewaunee lighthouse, back on shore is the Pioneer Park beach with over 500 feet of shoreline, and at the south end of the beach, Selner Park sits atop the beginning of the south

Kayak Wisconsin, Door County Peninsula

sandy bluff with a short path to the beach to launch your kayak.

North we go, and immediately the sandy bluffs tower on the shoreline. The scalloped edged bluffs rise to 60-70 feet and fall steeply down to the pebble beach shoreline. These beautiful bluffs were deposited by the Glacial period 20,000 to 30,000 years ago and were part of the Kewaunee glacial lobe. Lake Michigan itself is a large kettle lake formed as the retreating glacier scoured the land leaving the hole that the melting ice filled in, perhaps that is why its average temperature is about 50 degrees—refreshing!

Bluffs, Beaches, Lighthouses and Shipwrecks

The Kewaunee bluffs are blonde sand topped with rich forest green grass and woodlands which at times cascade down to water's edge. The light sandy bluffs contrast brilliantly with the twinkling blue waves. Beneath us, the crystal clear waters shine on the rocky lake bottom, so translucent that we head out further just to see how deep we can go and still see the gorgeous bottom! A gregarious grebe dives and ducks under and around our kayaks for a while. He is a small brown water bird with a short thick bill with his lobed feet far back on his body, perfect for bobbing around us.

Picture perfect paddling! The long line of steep curving sandy bluffs continue up the coast three miles to Mashek Creek. Here we land for a chance to explore this new and undeveloped public lands. The 1664 foot shoreline is wooded as Mashek Creek winds its way down the embankment to a pebble beach. This is a needed stopping point for migratory birds, and the creek fosters runs of salmon and trout. Quiet, tranquil area gave us a chance to stretch our legs and enjoy the rocky shoreline with the maple, oaks, and white birches leaning over the water's edge. This site is eventually planned to be a kayak and canoe launch site.

It's time to paddle on, with the windswept bluffs above us, and the clean clear water below. To the west of us lies Alaska Lake and we are nearing the old forgotten location of the Alaska Pier built in 1860 for the lumber schooners.

Soon Highway 42 comes to follow along our progress above the bluff. Wayside Park greets us with Three Mile Creek at its northern end. We land on the sandy beach and stroll to investigate the shoreline and the bubbling creek as it flows into Lake Michigan with its see-through, cold clean water. The Three Mile Creek winds its way from Krohns Lake west of Lake Michigan to Wayside Park. Guessing it twists and turns three miles, do ya think? Wayside Park also has historical significance with the Casco Pier built in 1860 for the lumber trade somewhere near here, lost and gone again. We throw out the beach blanket and settle in for our picnic lunch. "Wow, the forecast said 1-2 foot waves and we haven't even seen a white cap, wait—there's a white cap." Continue to enjoy our relaxed lunch, "boy the waves have picked up, wow, now there are a lot of white caps, guess that forecast was right."

During our relaxed shoreline lunch, the winds did begin to gust to 20 miles an hour, and our leisurely paddle has changed in intensity. Now we need to skirt up, tighten up our PFD's (lifejackets) and paddle hard off Wayside Park's beach and casual conversation turns to "great riding the wave" as we maintain our focus for the last three miles of our paddle with regular two foot waves coming directly from the east onto our starboard side. Soon Algoma's Pier head red Lighthouse beckons us, shall we head for the protected harbor or prove our ability and land on crescent beach (with folks watching from the boardwalk)? Who chose the beach??? Two foot crashing waves push us to shore threatening to twist us sideways, wait, "that one sounds huge, either we land on this wave or capsize". . . Land, we did—exciting! Paddle lift!!

Kayak Wisconsin, Door County Peninsula

Ah, then it hits us, we've completed our adventure. We've paddled from Green Bay, up the bay coast, around the tip of Wisconsin's thumb, through Death's Door, and down along Lake Michigan's shoreline to Kewaunee—directly east of Green Bay. Now what do we do?

Let's go celebrate! Algoma has the only winery we can actually paddle by. . .well perhaps not today, the waves are now reaching three to four foot crashing on shore, making it difficult even to talk. We'll walk the block to the Von Stiehl Winery. This winery is part of the Door Peninsula Wine Trail which includes the original winery, Door Peninsula Winery in Carlsville and offers over 50 fruit blend wines. Parallel 44 Winery is just down the road on Sleepy Hollow Road in Kewaunee on the 44 degree north latitude and specializes in wines with grapes grown in Wisconsin. There are two Sturgeon Bay Wineries, the Door 44 Winery (Parallel 44's sister winery,) and the Red Oak Vineyard offers red, white, dessert and cherry wines. The Harbor Ridge Winery in Egg Harbor is the newest winery with a sophisticated taste of artisan wine, while the Orchard County Winery in Fish Creek is in a restored dairy barn with winning wines from cherries, apples, grapes, raspberries and pears grown in their own orchard. If you are interested

Bluffs, Beaches, Lighthouses and Shipwrecks

in a wine making tour, then go to the Simon Creek Winery in Jacksonport which has the largest vineyard and most modern winery and offers wine making tours. Stone's Throw Winery in Baileys Harbor, offers wines made from premium California grapes made one barrel at a time, and if you would like something different, the Island Orchard Cider in Ellison Bay specializes in dry, crisp and refreshing rich ciders. But the Von Stiehl Winery in Algoma is the closest you'll come to kayaking up to a winery. Just a few feet from Crescent Beach, on the Algoma River, the winery is housed in a Civil War era building with limestone tunnels perfect for a winery and a spacious outdoor terrace with great Lake Michigan views, made for celebrating after completing our adventure circumnavigating the Door Peninsula!

What's next? Algoma and Kewaunee are trailheads for the Ahnapee Bike Trail. The Kewaunee section follows the Kewaunee River and then loops to Algoma where it follows the Ahnapee River and then curves north up the Door Peninsula to Sturgeon Bay. Heck, we could switch from paddling to pedaling and circumnavigate the Door Peninsula as land lovers.

Or, why not keep on paddling. The Lake doesn't end yet, right? Let's just keep on paddling south

Kayak Wisconsin, Door County Peninsula

along the Lake Michigan shoreline, heck Milwaukee is only a hundred some miles, and Chicago is only a wee bit further, less than a hundred miles down along the coast, then we could just curve back up the Michigan east side of the lake. . .

Paddle on, picture perfect paddling. . .

And always end with a paddle lift!

Bluffs, Beaches, Lighthouses and Shipwrecks

Logistics:

Directions to Crescent Beach in Algoma:

44.6063, -87.4357. OK, this one is easy. Crescent Beach is a half mile of sandy beach right on Highway 42 in downtown Algoma. The parking lot is at the north end of the beach next to the harbor. Restrooms are at end of Lake Street at the corner of Lake and Navarino Streets.

Directions to Wayside Park, south of Algoma:

44.5646, -87.4592. Again easy, Wayside Park is on the lakeshore off of Highway 42, 3.2 miles south of Algoma. Restrooms, tiny path down to beach–would be a difficult kayak/canoe launch.

Directions to Mashek Creek Recreation Area:

44.5021, -87.4840. From Highway 42, turn east on 1st toward Lake Michigan, in ¾ of a mile, the road curves north and turns into Lakeshore Drive, immediately to the right is Mashek Creek Recreation Area with a small path into the land. No fee, no restrooms, no developed kayak/canoe launch yet.

Directions to Father Marquette Memorial Park in Kewaunee:

44.4645, -87.4959. From Highway 42 in downtown Kewaunee, turn east on Hathaway Drive just north of the Kewaunee River. Father Marquette Memorial Park is at the intersection of Hathaway Drive and Lakeshore Drive. Parking lot, restrooms, no fee, protected kayak/canoe launch.

Directions to Kewaunee Boat Landing:

44.4637, -87.5045. From Highway 42 in downtown Kewaunee, turn west on Peterson Street and head into the parking lot to the farthest west boat launch for the kayak/canoe launch. Fee, restrooms.

Directions to Pioneer Park in Kewaunee:

44.4569, -87.4992. From Highway 42 in downtown Kewaunee (Main St, turns into Milwaukee St south of the bridge), turn eat at the third intersection south of the Kewaunee River on Kilbourn Street. Pioneer Park is at the end of

Kilbourn Street, turnaround at the end of the street. No fee, restrooms nearby.

Directions to Selner Park in Kewaunee:

44.4559, -87.4999. From Highway 42 in downtown Kewaunee, turn east on Vliet Street, parking lot is at the end of the street. No fee, restrooms nearby.

Kayak Wisconsin, Door County Peninsula

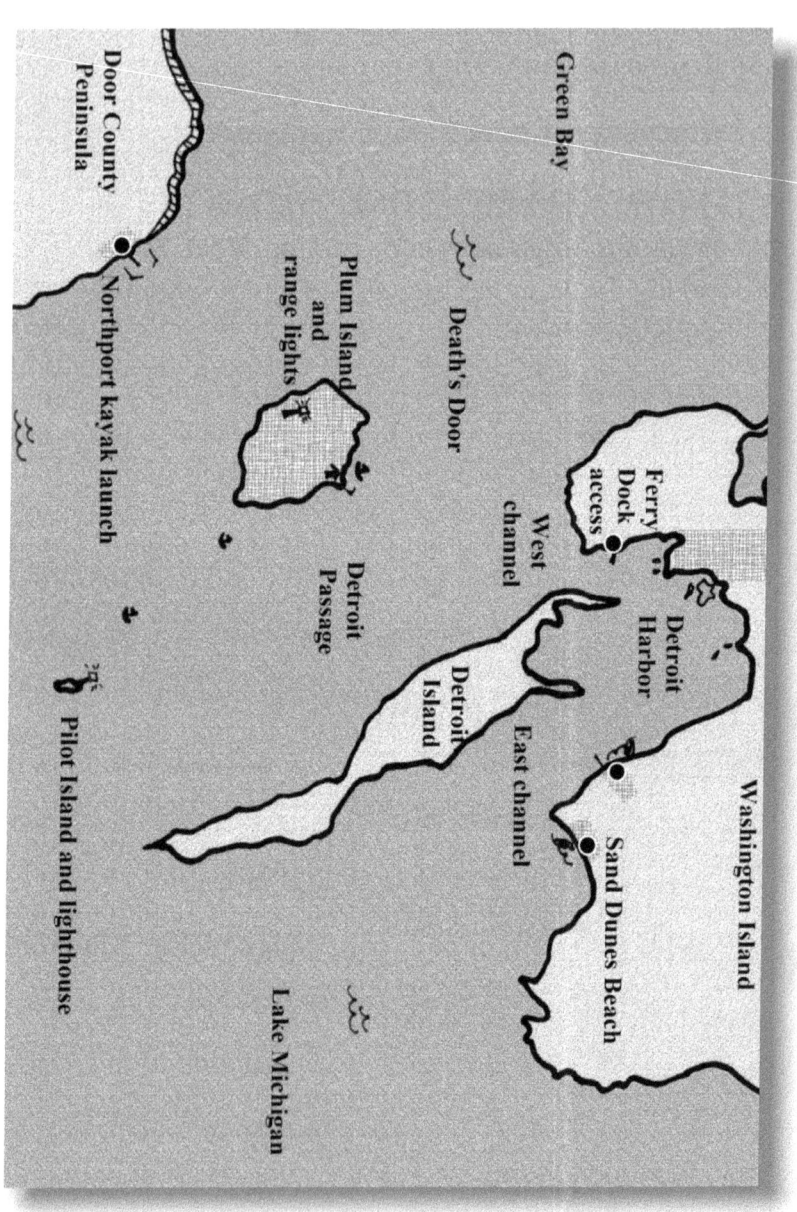

Bluffs, Beaches, Lighthouses and Shipwrecks

Bonus Island Paddle

Crossing Deaths Door

Northport to Plum, Pilot and Detroit Islands and to Washington Island

With Plum Island range lights and shipwreck, Pilot Island's lighthouse, and Detroit Island
11.5 miles

Port des Mort, Death's Door, be sure before you go. There is that mystique of Death's Door. If you are just interested in the bragging rights and an "I crossed Death's Door" t-shirt, you could bee line paddle across Death's Door in 5 miles but you'd miss the uniqueness of the islands. This paddle is a zigzag tour of the islands on our way over to Washington Island, across Death's Door. From the beach at Northport, paddle towards the Plum Island range lights and cruise over the lagoon shipwreck, then zag southeast towards the ghostly Pilot Island lighthouse, twist north and skim along the eastern shore of Detroit Island. Hop on over to Washington Island for a stretch, swim and picnic at Sand Dunes Beach. What to do on Washington Island without a paddle, err. . . wheels? No problem, head to the Washington Island Ferry dock and be whisked back to the mainland by the ferry!

Kayak Wisconsin, Door County Peninsula

Crossing Death's Door is not the longest crossing we've made, nor the coldest, nor the waviest, but something in the name Port des Morts, door way to death. . . makes one a tiny bit more edgy. The quiet waters that we can see past the Northport breakwater are notorious for changing their mind from the gentleness we see today to treacherous, violent clashing waves as the wind picks up. Here the currents of Lake Michigan meet the currents of Green Bay and they don't always play well together.

The passage is narrow and has many rocky shoals that wrecked havoc on the old time schooners, and the small canoes of the Native Americans before them. Actually the term Death's Door comes from the oral history of the Potawatomi and Winnebago people and a great battle fought from Washington Island to the Door County Peninsula in the 1640's where 600 warriors perished in a storm during the battle. Shortly after that the population of the Winnebago's plummeted and the name Death's Door was born.

The sparkly, glistening waters we paddle into have continued the tradition of the door way to death, as Door County owns more shipwrecks than any other body of fresh water. Le Griffen, was a 17th century barque schooner with three masts and square rigging built by the famous

Bluffs, Beaches, Lighthouses and Shipwrecks

Robert La Salle, searching for a passage way to China and Japan. Le Griffin made its maiden journey into Lake Michigan and to Washington Island in 1679, the first ship to ever traverse the Great Lakes. She unfortunately disappeared after leaving Washington Island and has never been found…Or has she? At times, she has been seen as a phantom ship in fog still sailing near Washington Island and the doorway to death, Death's Door. . .

And here we go, paddling into the door of death— OK, today it is a glorious sunny day with literally no waves as we glide towards Plum Island. The bright sunshine dispels all the ghost stories told over campfires. We speed along as Plum Island comes closer and closer, seems only a little jump across the water to Plum Island. Plum Island is truly less than two miles from Northport on Door County's mainland. It blocks the straight as a bird flies paddle to Washington Island, but that is OK, as it is a pretty little island. Plum is a tree covered island a speck more than one mile long and less than one mile wide. Perhaps the name is a tribute to its plum like shape, or perhaps like the rest of the islands and the Door County Peninsula, the soil of Plum Island was great for growing fruits— like perchance plums?

Kayak Wisconsin, Door County Peninsula

There must have been something to all the shipwreck stories, since Plum Island had its first lighthouse by 1845. That lighthouse proved to be ineffective, so the lighthouse was moved to Pilot Island. In 1872 alone, a hundred ships were stranded or damaged in Death's Door and in 1880 thirty boats were driven ashore at Plum Island. So by 1895, it was decided that Plum Island again needed a lighthouse. We first can see the larger sixty-five foot tall white back range light protruding above the tree line. It is a shiny white square iron skeleton pyramid eight feet in diameter with a center post with a circular staircase inside, topped with a circle watch room and an octagonal lantern room. The light still is a fourth order medium sized Fresnel lens which can be seen for thirteen miles. The front red range light is smaller with a square base and an octagonal second story lantern room with only one window with a red sixth order, smaller Fresnel light. Near the back white range light is the brick cream colored light keepers house, now waiting for help and restoration as all the structures on Plum Island are on the National Registry of Historic Places.

As we round the north point of Plum Island, a large vivid white building pops out against the deep forest green of Plum Island with the indigo

Bluffs, Beaches, Lighthouses and Shipwrecks

blue sky above. This is the newly painted white old Life Saving Station, affectionately called "the old guard" built in 1896 and in use for almost a century when the US Coast Guard moved to Washington Island in 1990. Plum and Pilot Islands are now owned by the US Fish and Wildlife Services and are part of the Green Bay Wildlife Refuge. Excitingly, the friends of Plum Island have opened up the island and shoreline to the public, with day access to the old Life Saving Station.

Paddle into Plum Island's lagoon and eight hundred feet before arriving at the Life Saving Station harbor wall, and four hundred feet off shore, lays the remains of an unidentified shipwreck thought to be the schooner Grapeshot which washed ashore in a November storm in 1867. She is easily seen and worth the effort to enjoy the harbor, lagoon and float over the shipwreck.

Leave the old guard and harbor behind and hug the shoreline to enjoy the rocky bluffs interspersed with cobblestone shorelines. We are now in Detroit Passage, between Detroit and Plum Islands. It is a fairly shallow passage with a middle shoal, which is, well, in the middle of the passage. As you paddle past the southeast point of Plum Island, look down for the Resumption shipwreck. She was a three masted schooner built in Milwaukee stranded near Plum Island in 1914 and lies in 20 feet of water. Shucks, we did not find her.

We pick up speed and skim over the surface of Lake Michigan and turn our attention towards Pilot Island. The little fleck of land lays about two miles off to the south east of Plum Island in line with the southern tip of Detroit Island. It is only about 500 feet long and 250 feet wide. But the island was a better location for a lighthouse than Plum Island as it is the gateway to Deaths Door from Lake Michigan. In 1858, the cream colored two and a half story light keepers home was built on the tallest rock on the island, a whopping eleven feet above the lake level. The home had a square tower with a ten sided decagonal cast iron lantern room with a fourth order Fresnel lens. A fog siren was added, as the little island was often shrouded in bleak mist. A dreary place it must have been, for one of the light keepers slit his own throat committing suicide, and another likened it to worse than Libby prison as the seas were often too rough to travel off the island. The name of this scrap of rock was initially called Port du Morts which is telltale today, as all the trees are dead, nude and covered in guano from the cormorants, gulls, and perhaps

a raven, that are now the only living souls on the island. Although the lighthouse was automated with a plastic lens in 1962, she is a shining beacon of safety for all who dare to enter the door to death. . . .Port du Morts.

Enough of the Edgar Allan Poe poetry, for evermore. . . Pilot Island is famous for shipwrecks and heroic rescues. At least ten shipwrecks were stranded by Pilot Island between 1858 and 1899. Martin Knudson, light house keeper on Pilot Island, risked his life to rescue the crew in the dark black night after hearing the crash of the A. P. Nichols as it was blown onto the rocks of his island in 1892. The A.P Nichols literally smashed into the year old wreck of the Forest, another three masted schooner. Light keeper Knudson used the wreck of the Forest to save the crew of the A.P. Nichols. The A.P. Nichols joined the J.E. Gilmore schooner which ran aground on Pilot Island only eleven days earlier. All three are now part of the Pilot Island Northwest Shipwreck Site and are on the National Register of Historic Places. They are down under thirty-five feet of water, probably too deep to see as we paddle by, but hats off to Knudson, the recipient of a gold medal for his heroism.

We zigzag north now en route to the lushness of Detroit Island's evergreens. Martin Knudson's son aptly called this string of islands "the stepping stones of Paul Bunyan". We are mighty Paul Bunyan is his kayak shoes stepping from island to island on this day trip. Step next to Detroit Island which was initially called Fallons Island after a crew member of the schooner Washington, one of the first ships to shelter at Washington Island. Detroit Island is a skinny four mile long strip of land propelling us into Detroit Harbor of Washington Island with two crab like tentacles at the north end. All of Detroit Island is private with no paved road or public accesses along the striking rock shelf boulder strung shoreline. The island is rumored to have been a hideout for natives when under attack by marauding tribes. It is also the thought to be the first attempt of white men to build a log cabin settlement. But in 1835, they were attacked and run off. It is easy to visualize a Native American behind each tree, bow and arrow in hand, defending his land as we paddle towards Detroit Harbor.

About half way up Detroit Island's northern side and at the little bay that dips in at the narrowest width of the island, detour north to Washington Island and the Sand Dunes Park. This is our favorite beach on Washington Island, a long carry in for a kayak launch, but the picturesque sand dune shoreline is a delight. The park has a quarter mile of shoreline with dune grass extending into the harbor. It's an impressive place to spread out the picnic blanket, OK, it does offer picnic tables, but the blanket is more charming on the mounds of sand waves. Time for lunch, time for reflection, time for. . .

Push off of Sand Dunes Park beach on Washington Island and cross Detroit Harbor's east channel. Hop past Rabbit Point, Detroit Island's northeast rabbit ear and through Pedersens Bay— the bay between Detroit Island's two north rabbit ears. 'Round Richters Point, Detroit Island's northwest tentacle and travel the west channel, sharing it with the ferry boats.

Kayak Wisconsin, Door County Peninsula

Head straight across the little west channel to the ferry dock. Follow the big brown harbor wall with the nice sitting benches above to the grassy incline just south of the wall. This is the designated kayak take out spot. It's a short carry to the ferry boat queue, and kind of fun to stand in the car line with your kayaks for the next ferry. The ferry boat crew is extremely pleasant and helpful and directed us to the most protected area for our boats on board the ship. They even lent a hand to carry our bags.

It is a quick breezy journey back by the motor boat ferry. Relive the Deaths Door passage as we are whisked back to the mainland. Feel the history along Detroit Island western shore, tour past Plum Island and its range lights, and view Pilot Island's mournful lighthouse. Ahh, then Northport's rocky breakwater welcomes us home safely.

We crossed Death's Door! Cheers! Time for a selfie!

Bluffs, Beaches, Lighthouses and Shipwrecks

Logistics:

Directions to Northport kayak launch:

45.2902, -86.9769. Couldn't be any easier. Take Highway 42 north until it ends at the ferry dock. Look to the east side of the harbor for the kayak launch.

Directions to Sand Dunes Beach Park, Washington Island:

45.3367, -86.8977 on Washington Island's south shore about 1/4 mile east from Detroit Harbor's eastern point in a little bay. If you were arriving by car, here are the driving directions: From Washington Island's ferry dock, take Lobdell Road northwest and follow it as it curves east for about 1.5 miles. At the intersection of Main Road, continue straight on Detroit Harbor Road (County Highway W) for about 1 mile, follow the curve as County Highway W curves east on Homestead Lane for 900 feet. Turn south on Range Line road, still County Highway W for .7 mile, which turns into South Shore Drive. At about .75 miles, there is a small parking area with a park sign on the right.

Kayak Wisconsin, Door County Peninsula

Directions to Washington Island's Ferry Dock Access:

45.3382, -86.9382 on Washington Island's southwestern corner, in Detroit Harbor north of Lobdell Point and just across from Richter Point of Detroit Island. Driving directions: From Main Road turn west on Detroit Harbor Road, turn southwest on Lobdell Point Road and follow it's curves for 1.5 miles to the Ferry Dock.

Shipwreck location:

Plum Island Lagoon shipwreck: 45.3138, -86.9515. tentatively identified as the schooner Grapeshot lies just off short 800 feet northwest of the Life Saving Harbor wall.

Resumption: stranded near Plum Island in 20 feet of water. We didn't find her. Good luck.

Pilot Island Shipwrecks: A.P. Nichols, Gilmore, and the Forest. Lie in 35 feet of water northwest of Pilot Island, probably not visible by kayak.

Kayak Wisconsin, Door County Peninsula

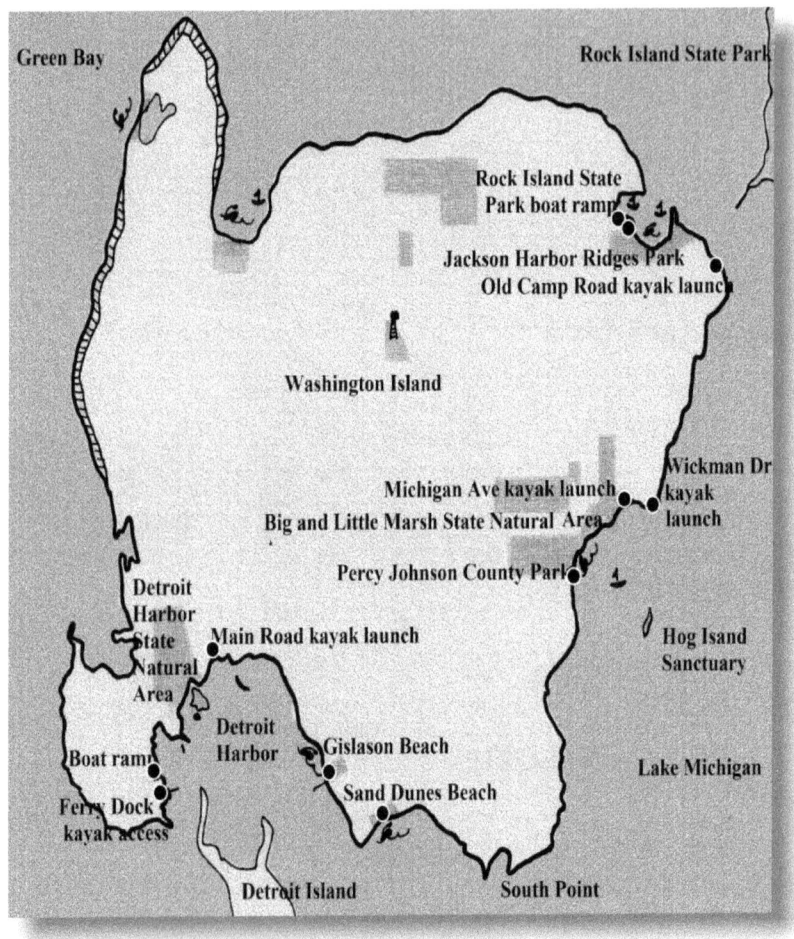

Bonus Island Paddle

Washington Island Lakeside

Ferry dock kayak access to Jackson Harbor Ridges Park
With Gislason, Sand Dunes, and Percy Park Beaches, and several shipwrecks
11 miles

Relax. . . you are north of the tension line, as WashingtonIsland.com boasts. This peaceful paddle takes you through the southern shoreline of Washington Island's Detroit Harbor with stops at several pleasant beaches, then round South Point and up the lakeside. Enjoy Hog Island's bird sanctuary, head north around Calvin Point and into Jackson Harbor to Ridges Park. Oh, and be on the lookout for the rubble of three sunken shipwrecks. . .

There are lots of kayak access points on the lower lakeside of Washington Island. Divide this paddle into two tranquil days of paddling at Percy Johnson County Park almost half way up the eastern side of the island, giving yourself the gift of two tension free days: a beaches and then a lakeside day.

Washington Island is the largest of the Grand Traverse string of islands connecting mainland

Kayak Wisconsin, Door County Peninsula

Wisconsin to the Upper Peninsula of Michigan. From the tip of Wisconsin's Door Peninsula paddle north to Plum, Detroit, Washington, and Rock Island, then into Michigan for St Martin, Poverty, Summer and Little Summer Islands finally arriving at Upper Michigan's Garden Peninsula approximately thirty three miles later. This is the Niagara Escarpment jutting out of the water every couple of miles.

Start your day off the southern steep natural shoreline next to the Ferry Dock wall, or north a bit at the public boat landing. Sweep past this busy boat area and sooth into the Detroit Harbor State Natural Area. Float past Little and Big Susie Islands exploring for migratory birds stopping over, including terns, ducks, eagles and white pelicans. The Richter bayou is here with ground water springs creating a natural smallmouth bass nursery through the network of channels and wetlands. The Detroit Harbor State Natural Area provides a nice insight into the terrain and abundance of wildlife that the Potawatomi Native Americans found so inviting. Washington Island's first known name was Wassekiganeso, an Ojibwe Potawatomi name loosely translated into "shining cliffs".

In the bowl of the bay of Detroit Harbor, the southern end of Main Road offers a kayak access or resting spot. From here you can wiggle your way around tree studded Snake Island. Jean Nicolet was the first early explorer to discover Washington Island in 1635. Explorers gave the island the name Washington when they sailed into one of its harbors on the flagship schooner "The Washington".

On the eastern shore of Detroit Harbor is our first beach, Gislason Beach. Jon Gislason, was one of the first Icelander's to settle on the island. Washington Island now has one of the oldest and largest Icelandic heritage in the United States. Gislason Beach and Red Barn Park was originally a noted local store in 1885 and is now a Community Center. The wonderfully restored beach with the gentle sloping soft sand beach with the rustling beach grasses is nicely protected by Rabbit Point of Detroit Island just a half mile hop off shore. This park is actually a thirteen acre tract of land with a natural hiking path into the island's topography.

Next door to Gislason Beach is the popular Sailors Pub restaurant known for great food with exceptional sunset views. It is one of the few restaurants on Washington Island actually on the shoreline.

Kayak Wisconsin, Door County Peninsula

Our next beach is less than a mile of lily dip paddling around the little point at the eastern end of Detroit Harbor. Soon the sand dunes peek out on the shoreline. Sand Dunes beach is one of our favorite beaches on the island with its 1200 feet of sandy ridge shoreline to explore. From the parking area on South Shore Drive, it is a long boat carry of 500 feet over deep soft sand to the dune shoreline, but by kayak it is a delightful stop on our paddle. It is exactly the high mounded bank of smooth sand box like sand that makes this beach beloved. At water's edge the dune grasses wrestle with the waves to hold the sand ashore as we wade out for a swim. The view westward is of Detroit Island greenery just a mile across the blue harbor. Eastward is South Point evergreens sprinkled with white birch trees above the whistling dune grasses.

Paddle east and around Washington Island's South Point with its deep green woodland. Enjoy this last greenery before Lake Michigan's 53 miles of fresh water sea before reaching Lower Michigan's shore. We take an "oh my God" moment for the spacious vista of this beautiful body of water we have been exploring. Lake Michigan seems never ending with the shimmering sapphire blue water speckled with sunlight off the tips of the waves

fading to the far horizon with the powder blue sky fanning out in all directions. Ahh. . .we truly are north of the tension line.

'Rounding South Point, we begin paddling north along the eastern coast of Washington Island. This side of the island is forested, with cottage homes peeking out of the trees. White cedar is prominent, but you will also find balsam fir, tamarack, and hemlocks.

Point your bow towards Hog Island, a narrow strip of island which is a wildlife refuge and nesting area for terns and gulls. Cruise by slowly to enjoy the flight and fancy of this large family of birds amongst the boulders and shrubs on the island. Float to the inside of Hog Island and search for the remains of the two-masted schooner, Winfield Scott, which capsized and drifted onto these rocks. She lies broken and scattered on both sides of the north tail of the island as it drifts under water. You'll find the pieces of the Winfield Scott about a third of a mile off shore of Lake View Road.

Now would be a wonderful time for a lunch break, so head just north of Lake View Road to Percy Johnson County Park. It is a nice park with grills, picnic tables, and…restrooms. Percy Johnson Park offers two hundred feet of shoreline to explore. Off shore is a sandy and cobblestone mixed beach bottom. Along the coastline you'll find slender soft stemmed bog arrow grass and long leafed bulrushes that filter and help reduce water pollution. Search also for the endangered vibrant deep blue dwarf lake iris, and perhaps you'll spy a mermaid. . .the delicate feathery false mermaid weed.

Inland from the park, is the Big and Little Marsh State Natural Area. The marshes are natural aquatic fens—mineral rich earthy wetlands. Along the shores of the marshes is part of Wisconsin's boreal forest, the second largest in the world. Here you'll find the exchange of energy and water as the trees transition from southern to northern trees. In the Big and Little State Natural

Bluffs, Beaches, Lighthouses and Shipwrecks

Area the white cedars, balsam firs and hemlocks co-mingle with the white spruce and birch trees, all giving off that magical "up north" scent.

Just north of Percy Johnson County Park, after a few private homes, is a natural area on the shore and this is the Little Marsh State Natural Area. Feel free to land and take a whiff of the wonderful boreal forest pine smell, another reminder that you are north of the tension line. . . A speck north of this, Michigan Road peeks out, and after just a quarter mile more is the end of Wickman Drive, both easy public access points.

We paddle north along this sunrise coast on our super sunny summer day. As we paddle, we can't see where Washington Island ends and Rock Island begins, they are that close together. At Old Camp Road, another scenic put in or rest spot, we finally can tell that Rock Island is literally only about a half mile away as Washington Island's northeastern shoal stretches towards Rock Island's southern tail.

Go around the northern tip of Washington Island and cross the sandy shoal. All of Carlin's Point, the eastern point of Jackson Harbor is part of Jackson Harbor Ridges State Natural Area. Land, explore, and enjoy the exquisite view across to Rock Island's gleaming white Viking Hall

Boathouse. As we go into Jackson Harbor along the inside of Carlin's Point, investigate the sunken remains of the Kate William, a steam tug stranded in 1907 on the beach in Jackson Harbor on the inside of the eastern knoll. Poor Kate is broken up and scattered to kingdom come. . .all right, she is scattered all the way to Rock Island. She is easily found just 60 feet off shore in about two feet of water.

Cross Jackson Harbor and land on the beach by Jackson Harbor Ridges Park by the little ice house, across the road from Jackson Harbor's Maritime Museum in the fishing sheds. The ice house is a quaint example of Wisconsin's winter harvest of lake ice. The ice was cut into 18 inch by 36 inch cakes, floated to shore in ice channels, pushed up on shore, and brought to the ice house by a team of horses. Surrounded by saw dust, the ice blocks would survive into the summer to refrigerate the "ice boxes" in our ancestor's homes.

The alternative take out spot is the public boat ramp at the end of Rock Island State Park Road. This gives you the opportunity to search for the shipwreck of the Iris, a two-masted flat bottomed scow schooner with a square bow. The Iris ran aground in 1913 in about two feet of water between the State Park boat ramp and the commercial fishing docks. Her straight and high rudder shoe is the easiest to spot. She is on Wisconsin's National Register of Historic places.

Now if you only brought one car and planned ahead with a reserved site, you could cross over to Rock Island and camp. Or if you are not a camper, then the Jackson Harbor Inn is just a short carry up Jackson Harbor Road by the Jackson Harbor Ridges State Natural Area. Just look'n for a snack. . .the Time Out Concessions stand at the Jackson Harbor Maritime Museum offers hotdogs, brats, sandwiches and munchies.

Logistics:

Directions to Washington Island Ferry kayak access:

45.3382, -86.9382.

Take the Washington Island Ferry across Deaths Door and when you exit the boat, look south and at the end of the metal wall there is a steep incline that is the kayak access. There are restrooms in the ferry building, no fee.

Kayak Wisconsin, Door County Peninsula

Directions to Washington Island Detroit Harbor public boat ramp:

45.3402, -86.9386. 284 Lobdell Point Road. From the Washington Island Ferry dock, take the curve right onto Lobdell Point Road (Highway W) and in 300 feet, across from the Welcome Center, turn right down to the public boat ramp.

Directions to Main Road public access:

45.3529, -86.9298. 723 Main Road. From the Washington Island Ferry dock, take Lobdell Point Road (Highway W) to the right for 1.7 miles and turn right/south on Main Road .2 miles. There is parking on the shoulder of the road. No restrooms, no fees.

Directions to Gislason Public Beach and access:

45.3403, -86.9089. 1483 South Shore Drive. From the Washington Island Ferry dock, take Highway W/Lobdell Point Road to the right for 2.8 miles, continue left on Highway W/Homestead Lane for .2 miles, then right on Highway W/Range Line Road for .7 miles, beach is on the right as the road curves and turns into

Bluffs, Beaches, Lighthouses and Shipwrecks

South Shore Drive. Restrooms available across the road, no fees.

Directions to Sand Dunes Beach and public access:

45.3367, -86.8977. 1284 South Shore Drive. From the Washington Island Ferry dock, take Highway W/Lobdell Point Road to the right for 2.8 miles, continue left on Highway W/Homestead Lane for .2 miles, then right on Highway W/Range Line Road which turns into South Shore Drive for 1.4 miles. Parking area is on the right side of the road. Long (500 feet) sandy carry to beach. Restrooms available, no fees.

Directions to Percy Johnson County Park:

45.3636, -86.8643. 640 Lake View Road. From the Washington Island Ferry dock, take Highway W/Lobdell Point Road to the right for 1.7 miles, turn left on Main Road for .4 miles and at the third right turn right onto Lake View Road and follow it to Lake Michigan for 3.2 miles to Percy Johnson Eastside County Park. There is a parking lot, restrooms and no fees!

Kayak Wisconsin, Door County Peninsula

Directions to Michigan Road public access:

45.3698, -86.8549. 460 Michigan Road. From the Washington Island Ferry dock, take Highway W/Lobdell Point Road to the right for 1.7 miles, turn left on Main Road for .8 miles, then right on Michigan Road for 3.6 miles to the end at Lake Michigan. Parking on the shoulder of the road, no restrooms, no fees.

Directions to Wickman Drive public access:

45.3696, -86.8501. 359 Wickman Road. From the Washington Island Ferry dock, take Highway W/Lobdell Point Road to the right for 1.7 miles, turn left on Main Road for .8 miles, then right on Michigan Road for 3.6 miles, then left on Wickman Road for .4 miles, at the T intersection take a sharp right on Wickman Road for 150 feet to the lake shore. Parking on the shoulder of the road, no restrooms, no fees.

Directions to Old Camp Road Washington Island public access:

45.3960, -86.8393. From Washington Island's ferry dock, turn north on Lobdell Point Rd/County Road W for 1.7 miles, then turn north on Main Road (which happens to continue to be County

Road W) drive 2.6 miles, turn right on Jackson Harbor Road (which interestingly enough continues to be County Road W) for 3.5 miles, continue straight on Old Camp Road for .6 miles, at the T intersection turn left to stay on Old Camp Road for .3 miles, and then turn right to stay on Old Camp Road for .4 miles to Lake Michigan. No fee, no restrooms.

Directions to Jackson Harbor Ridges Park:

45.3997, -86.8547. 1899 Jackson Harbor Road. From Washington Island's ferry dock, turn north on Lobdell Point Rd/County Road W for 1.7 miles, then turn north on Main Road/ County Road W drive 2.6 miles, turn right on Jackson Harbor Road/County Road W for 3.7 miles, turn right to stay on Jackson Harbor Road for .2 miles until you see the beach access on the right. There is a parking lot, no restrooms, no fees.

Directions to Rock Island State Park boat launch:

45.3995, -86.8547. Rock Island State Park Road. From Washington Island's ferry dock, turn north on Lobdell Point Rd/County Road W for 1.7 miles, then turn north on Main Road/County Road

Kayak Wisconsin, Door County Peninsula

W drive 2.6 miles, turn right on Jackson Harbor Road/County Road W for 3.7 miles, turn left onto Indian Point Road for .2 miles, then right onto Rock Island State Park Road to the boat launch. Parking lot available, restrooms available. Fee.

Shipwreck locations:

Winfield Scott: 45.3631,-86.8563 and 45.3615,-86.8553. A two masted schooner capsized and drifted onto the rocks and lies in about 6 feet of water on the north tail of Hog Island just off Lake View Drive.

Kate Williams: 45.4010, -86.8491 and new piece discovered 45.4031, -86.8374. A 2 steam tug, stranded in 1907 on the Jackson Harbor eastern knoll on beach in 2 feet of water, and out on the shoal between Jackson Harbor and Rock Island southern tip.

Iris: 45.4006, -86.8554. A two-masted flat bottomed scow schooner with a square bow ran aground in 1913 in about two feet of water between the State Park boat ramp and the commercial fishing docks.

Kayak Wisconsin, Door County Peninsula

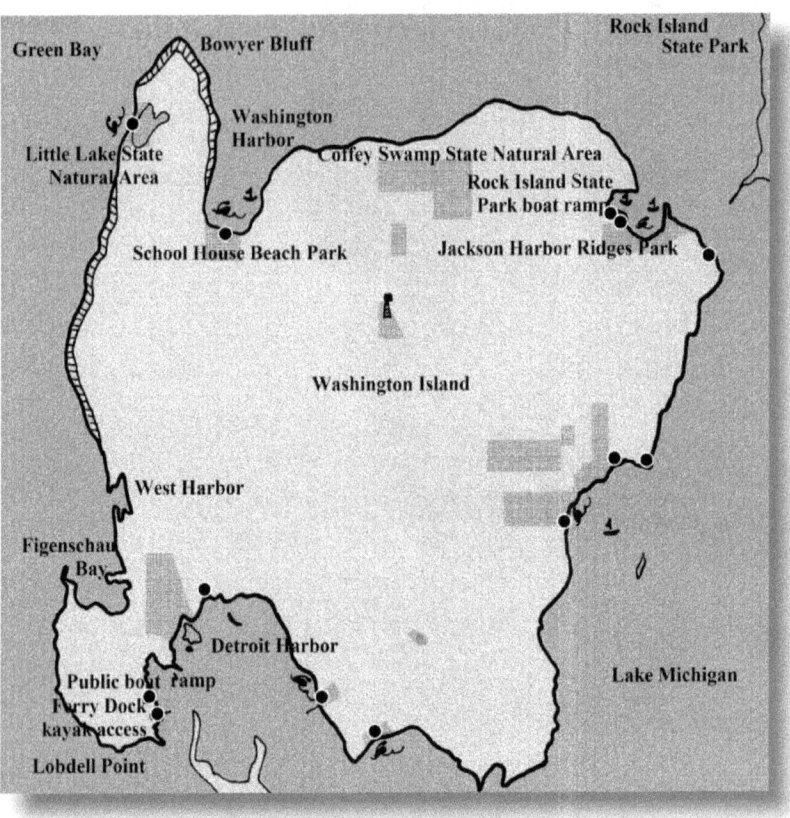

Bonus Island Paddle

Washington Island Bayside Bluffs

Jackson Harbor to Detroit Harbor
*With Schoolhouse Beach and shipwreck,
and the one and only Little Lake*
14 miles

Big. Bold. Beautiful Bluffs. Impressive bluffs, some of the best we've seen—certainly in the top five best bluffs in Door County. Add the stunning natural wonder of white flat stones, picture perfect beaches, and a silent sunken shipwreck, and you've got the Wow factor working.

Bit of a long paddle, but you are able to break it up into two wonderful days. Put in at Jackson Harbor Ridges Park and you could do a short day north side paddle to Schoolhouse Beach in Washington Harbor for a 5 mile paddle with time to enjoy the beach and shipwreck. That leaves a second day paddle from Schoolhouse Beach out of Washington Harbor around bountiful Bowyer Bluff with a rest break at Little Lake and down the western, Green Bay side of Washington Island, around Lobdell Point and into the western channel of Detroit Harbor to the ferry boat kayak access for a 9 plus mile paddle.

Kayak Wisconsin, Door County Peninsula

Launch in Jackson Harbor at Ridges Park for a soft shore push off with a view of the historic ice house shanty. The ice house exhibits how old Wisconsinites harvested Lake Michigan winter ice to keep their food cold in their non-electric ice boxes into summer.

Jackson Harbor Ridges State Natural area offers over a mile of shoreline with twelve sand ridges with low swales between, and special coastal rare flora including delicate blue kalms lobelia, shrubby cinquefoil with clusters of yellow flowers, five lobed purple birds-eye primrose, and light purple low calamint with a rich mint aroma. How about the carnivorous bladderwort? This sophisticated plant has floating yellow flowers above the water with air filled bladders under the water that traps protozoa swimming in the water saturated soil. The drier dunes show off rare creeping juniper, yellow daisyish sand coreopsis, downy dune thistle, yellow semi-evergreen dune goldenrod, and the white hairy sticky asphodel with small clumps of flowers turning to reddish capsule fruit. Look also for bear berry, a low growing evergreen with pale pink flowers in spring and red berries later. On the older dunes you'll see red pines, white pine and cedars, balsam fir, and beech trees. The Ridges Park is a great area for terns, gulls, and shorebirds. All in all, take your time getting into the water to enjoy this special protected area.

Stay close in by shore to tour past the Iris shipwreck between Jackson Harbor commercial fishing docks and Rock Island State Park boat ramp—your alternative launch site. The Iris was a two masted, flat bottomed, blunt bow scow schooner that ran aground in March 1913 and lies broken and buried in two feet of water just off shore. Even though it has been over a century, you can still see parts of her center board, outer hull, and rudder shoe.

Watch out for Karfi, the Rock Island ferry boat as you make your way out of Jackson Harbor. Enjoy the view across to Rock Island where the dramatic white Viking Hall boat house stands with her arched windows, a testament to the clear air with no exhaust fumes, since Rock Island allows no cars. Go around Indian Point, the western side of Jackson Harbor, to the north shore of Washington Island. Here we are in the lee as there is a strong due south wind a blow'n.

Midway of Washington Island's northern shoreline is a pristine natural area shoreline with beautiful rock ledge beaches graced with a boreal snow forest of pines and cedars. Behind this rocky shoreline lies Coffey Swamp State Natural

Kayak Wisconsin, Door County Peninsula

Area. This is a former shallow Lake Michigan bay with a freshwater pond fen with several peculiar plants. Here lives the glistening sundew plant that lures and absorbs insects on glands on its leaves, and the pitcher plant with its deeply folded goblet shaped leaves with sweet juice inside that traps insects to their deaths. Since we are not particularly fond of insects, we have a high regard for these plants. . .

No, don't do it, don't do it—don't be called by the beautiful bluff across the bay, you must, you must turn the corner into Washington Harbor. What makes it a harbor instead of a bay? Here is where Colonel Talbot Chambers hid from a big bad storm, on his way to Green Bay in 1816. He had three ships, some of the first huge sailing ships to sail the Great Lakes. His lead ship, his flagship, was called The Washington. Therefore he named the island and this protected bay, Washington Harbor.

But that is not the reason you need to explore this beautiful bay, err, harbor. Stay close to the eastern shoreline and start looking down beneath the waves at about a half mile. Here lies the Louisiana, who was not as lucky as Colonel Chamber's Washington ship at taking refuge. In the Great Storm of 1913 she ran aground dragging her anchor, and if that is not bad enough. . .caught

Bluffs, Beaches, Lighthouses and Shipwrecks

fire and sank. The crew was able to save themselves and make it ashore with their lifeboat. This November storm with seventy miles per hour wind, raged for four days and was responsible for sinking twenty vessels and killing scores of sailors. The Louisiana, a wood bulk steamer, has lain in her watery grave fairly intact for over a hundred years in fifteen feet of water with her bow ashore. The shoreline is private homes, so floating over her or swimming and snorkeling is the only way to see her.

Now paddle towards the white shoreline in the inner bay, less than a half mile away. This is the famed school house beach. School House beach is unique—there are only five like it in the whole world. It is not a soft sandy shore, but a spectacular smooth, small, white stone beach, a natural marvel. This geological wonder of

Kayak Wisconsin, Door County Peninsula

millions of sun warmed stones is even more striking as they extend under the crystal clear, turquoise lapping waves. The stones were created by tumbling in the waves, so go ahead and skip the stones, they'll return in an eon or so back to the beach. Create baby balanced stone piles, cairns—how high can you go? Walk the beach and enjoy the talking stones as they click clack together. No souvenirs please, you'll want to bring your grandchildren here some day.

The stones are glacial polished dolomite white limestone, but that lesson is not why this is called Schoolhouse Beach. In 1850, the first settlers built a log school house on Washington Island on this beach. Schoolhouse Beach is a delightful area for a picnic with the wooded area breaking out into that gorgeous bay vista with restrooms, grills and a soda/water machine. Also this is our take out spot if you chose the short day paddle.

Swim, relax, repeat. Is it time? Must we? Time to jump back into the kayaks and continue our exploration. . .but trust us, it's worth it. Head up the western shoreline of Washington Harbor. Watch as the bluffs grow, white stone beach below, soaring striated cliffs, and various filtering shades of pastel and emerald greens atop, cascading down and over the bluffs. It is less than two miles to the tip of Bowyer Bluff, but exquisitely enjoyable paddling. As we round the Bowyer Bluff point, view back into the harbor, then east to Rock Island, and then west to nothing—nothing but big indigo blue bay and pale baby blue sky. Way off on the horizon, almost twenty miles away, there are fluffy white clouds, signaling the change in atmosphere as the Green Bay fresh water meets mainland Upper Michigan.

Heading south along the western shoreline of Washington Island, the vivid white rocky pebble beach continues under the steep shear bluffs. Tufts of shrubbery make a hold in the cracks and crevices. Occasionally large boulders lie on the stony shore, remnants of cliff collapses.

In less than a mile we come to Little Lake. Stop, land, enjoy. . .it is a hidden jewel. Land on the pebble and rock beach where you can glimpse the lake over the slim cobblestone ridge separating Green Bay from Little Lake. This is the only, yes only, lake in Washington Island. It is a petite twenty-four acre lake, with a modest six foot depth. Most of the shoreline is undeveloped historically rich land now preserved by our friends at Door County Land Trust. Little Lake was once home to a large Native American village and burial ground and is now a preserved archeological state historical site. Many of the artifacts can be seen at the Jocabsen Museum and his olde vertical log cabin located on the south side of the lake. Little Lake is a pristine land locked lake that was formed from the receding glacial Lake Nippising. It has 1,300 feet of Green Bay shoreline with 53 acres of wetlands and forest. It is home to the marsh bell flower, dwarf iris, along with eagles, white pelicans and blue warblers. The lake offers perch and bass if you brought along your fishing pole. The walk in is one and a quarter miles from Main Road, a bit much for a kayak launch, but an awesome stop along the Green Bay shoreline for a peaceful, quiet rest break.

Back in our boats, we continue south along the bluff and cobblestone shoreline. However, we are now paddling directly into a stiff south wind creating two to three foot whitecaps. Attacking the waves head on, we charge along the shoreline. No rest, no stretch, no quick sip of water, or we are rewarded by being pushed back the many feet we just gained. Thankfully, the shoreline scenery is impressive. For over three hard fought nautical miles there are no public rest spots. There are several rental cottages and quaint resorts along the way and finally West Harbor offers refuge.

West Harbor with its superb limestone bluffs, is tucked into the shoreline and if you paddle early enough and arrive before 11:00 am, you are in time for a true Icelandic breakfast at Sunset Resort with Scandinavian pancakes filled with crème. Stay the night at a West Harbor resort to enjoy the "sunsets that become souvenirs" as the Gibson Resort advertises. There are beaches at the resorts for kayak launches so this makes it a wonderful way to paddle to the island and tour around it and stay at the resorts on the shoreline for a no car hassle. Before the Civil War, West Harbor also provided safe refuge for a runaway slave settlement.

Figenschau Bay is a larger bay created by the western club foot of Washington Island that provides us with an appreciated wind barrier of that never ending, crescendo building, whitecap action from that nasty ole south wind. The bay provides beautiful sheltered views of Green Bay.

Finally, we start rounding the southern west side of Washington Island and begin to get a slight block from the mainland Door County Peninsula. Pause and take pleasure in the magnificent panorama across Deaths Door, the volatile water between Washington Island and the Door County Peninsula, to Table Bluff and Northport three to four miles away. Relish the view of Deaths Door Island's: the deep evergreen of Plum Island just a mile and a half away, long sleek Detroit Island almost touchable at a half mile away, and the tiny blimp of Pilot Island in the distance at three and a quarter miles between the other two islands.

Paddle past the protective Potato Dock with its 600 foot extension, round Lobdell Point and turn into the western channel into Detroit Harbor. Stay close to the shoreline to avoid the ferry boats and tour past the new Coast Guard Station with its sky high tower while you peek over to the northeast side of Plum Island and the bright white "Old Guard" historic coast guard station.

Just after the private marina, land on the steep slope before the high brown metal break wall of the Ferry Dock. This is the public access for kayaks catching the ferry. If you prefer the public boat ramp, it is a block past the ferry dock.

Now if you ferried your vehicle over to the island, this would be a wonderful time to explore the interior of the island. Our recommendations may include the lavender farm and store where you can actually try lavender ice cream, or climb the 186 steps up the Mountain Lookout tower for a majestic view of where you just kayaked. Check out expert kayaker, Valerie Fons, kayak museum and learn from the expert. Think you can do a marathon paddle around Washington Island? The experts complete this paddle in three to four hours during the Door County Sea Kayak Symposium.

Bluffs, Beaches, Lighthouses and Shipwrecks

Are you ready for some rest and relaxation? Then join the Bitter's Club at Nelson's Pub, the oldest legal tavern in Wisconsin where Danish Tom Nelson was allowed to continue serving his 90 proof Angostura Bitters as a stomach tonic during Prohibition.

Per our plan, we are heading back to the mainland via the Washington Island ferry. Very exhausted, we felt a little silly sitting in line with our kayaks in the queue of cars waiting for the ferry. We cheered when our boat arrived, especially when the crew helped carry our kayaks and gear aboard! They knew to keep our bags in the rear, safely away from the rough sea splashing over the bow of the boat. We enjoyed the comfort of the ferry, just relaxing as we crossed Deaths Door with its now ominous looking four and five foot crashing waves. Glad we chose to safely ferry across, rather than paddle through Deaths Door which is named for its famed ability to seek out, destroy, and sink any vessel that thinks it can out whip Port des Morts. . .Deaths Door. . .

Kayak Wisconsin, Door County Peninsula

Logistics:

Directions to Jackson Harbor Ridges Park:

45.3997, -86.8547. 1899 Jackson Harbor Road. From Washington Island's ferry dock, turn north on Lobdell Point Rd/County Road W for 1.7 miles, then turn north on Main Road (which happens to continue to be County Road W) drive 2.6 miles, turn right on Jackson Harbor Road (which interestingly enough continues to be County Road W) for 3.7 miles, turn right to stay on Jackson Harbor Road for .2 miles until you see the beach access on the right. There is a parking lot, no restrooms, no fees.

Directions to Rock Island State Park boat launch:

45.3995, -86.8547. Rock Island State Park Road. From Washington Island's ferry dock, turn north on Lobdell Point Rd/County Road W for 1.7 miles, then turn north on Main Road (which happens to continue to be County Road W) drive 2.6 miles, turn right on Jackson Harbor Road (which interestingly enough continues to be County Road W) for 3.7 miles, turn left onto Indian Point Road for .2 miles, then right onto

Bluffs, Beaches, Lighthouses and Shipwrecks

Rock Island State Park Road to the boat launch. Parking lot available, restrooms available. Fee.

Directions to Schoolhouse Beach and kayak launch:

45.3982, -86.9274. 1860 Schoolhouse Beach Road. From Washington Island's ferry dock, turn north on Lobdell Point Rd/County Road W for 1.7 miles, then turn north on Main Road (which happens to continue to be County Road W) drive 2.6 miles, turn right on Jackson Harbor Road (which interestingly enough continues to be County Road W) for .2 miles, turn left at the second road- Schoolhouse Beach Road .2 miles, parking area to the left. No fees, restrooms available.

Directions to Washington Island Ferry kayak access:

45.3382, -86.9382.

Take the Washington Island Ferry across Deaths Door and when you exit the boat, look south and at the end of the metal wall there is a steep incline that is the kayak access. There are restrooms in the ferry building, no fee.

Kayak Wisconsin, Door County Peninsula

Directions to Washington Island Detroit Harbor public boat ramp:

45.3402, -86.9386. 284 Lobdell Point Road. From the Washington Island Ferry dock, take the curve right onto Lobdell Point Road (Highway W) and in 300 feet, across from the Welcome Center, turn right down to the public boat ramp.

<u>Shipwreck locations:</u>

Iris: 45.4006, -86.8554. A two-masted flat bottomed scow schooner with a square bow ran aground in 1913 in about two feet of water between the State Park boat ramp and the commercial fishing docks.

Louisiana: 45.4007,-86.9203. A wooden bulk steamer was blown ashore at anchor and caught fire while riding out the Great Storm of 1913 in Washington Harbor Washington Island. The Louisiana lies on shore and into 15 feet of water on the east side of Washington Harbor, less than a 1/2 mile from Schoolhouse Beach.

Kayak Wisconsin, Door County Peninsula

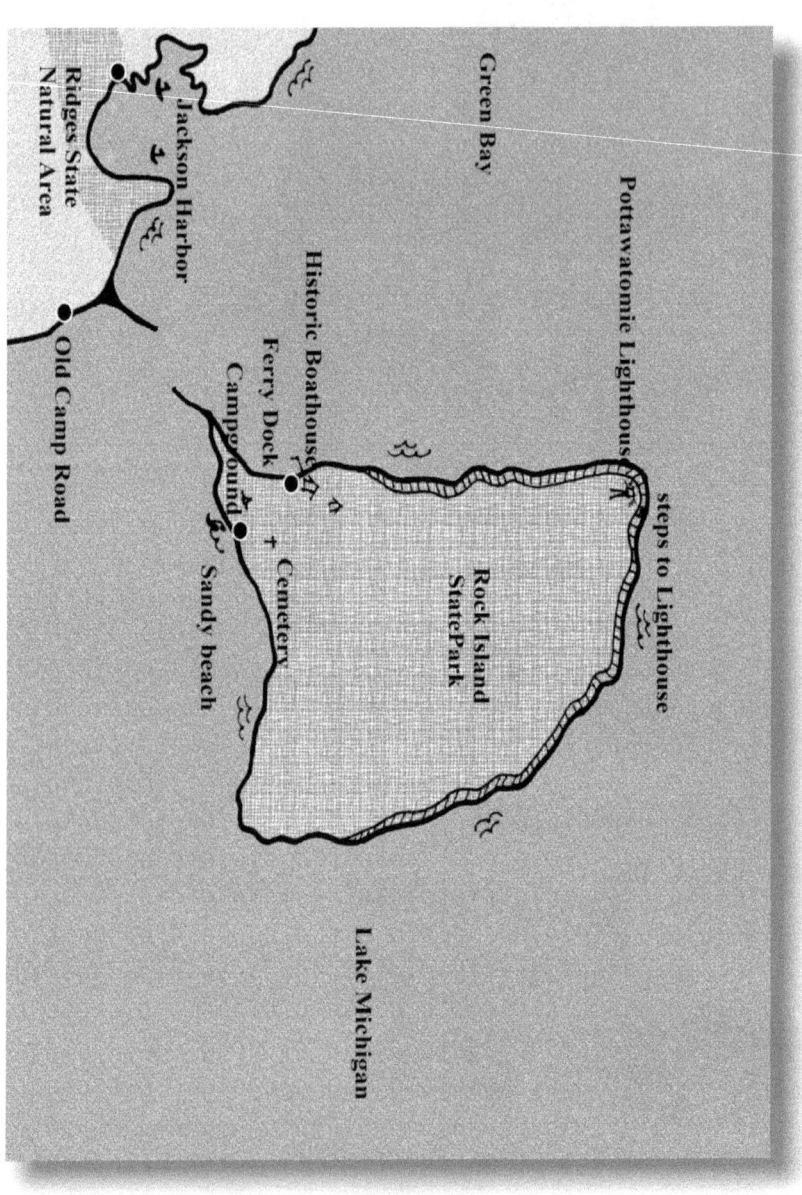

Bonus Island Paddle

Rock Island Naturally

Great circumnavigation paddle
With an expansive sand beach, sheer bluffs, and vivid white historic stone buildings
9 miles

Now we know, now we know. . .why it is called Rock Island and why folks are drawn to it and circumnavigate around the island by kayak. It's a majestic huge rock with a top hat of white cedars. Start on the south bottom of the rock triangle with the sandy shore. Follow the sandy shore and watch as it slowly grows and matures into beautiful sea carved bluffs. Turn around the eastern edge of the triangle and watch in awe as it bursts into the regal imposing massive sheer cliff at the northern tip of the rock and sail down the western cliff side and ending back at the southwest long tip with the white limestone historic estate buildings.

Don't bother with the passenger only ferry, no cars, no bikes, but that is exactly what makes Rock Island special—it's primitive. Maybe you could bring your kayaks on the ferry, depends on how busy and how many passengers, kinda iffy, and it is only a one mile crossing over to Rock

Island. Therefore we recommend kayaking out to Rock Island from Washington Island. Put in at Jackson Harbor Ridges State Natural area or for even a shorter crossing, launch at the Old Camp Road public access. Both sites are located on the northeastern tip of Washington Island. Follow the sandy shoal that snakes its way to the southwest lip of Rock Island.

Stop any time along the sandy beach on the bottom of Rock's triangle. Rock Island is famous for this half mile of sand beach. This is where the only really accessible by kayak campsites are located. Enjoy the beach and search for the rock carvings created by an Icelandic wood carver. We enjoyed a little nap on our beach blanket after our paddle to the island and watched several groups of kayakers circumnavigating the island. The wind from the south had picked up and whitecaps were crashing on the shore, this was definitely not the lee side of the island. Please be safe, please be safe.

When the sandy shore ends, the bluffs begin. There are five walk in primitive wilderness campsites along the southeast tip of the island. Ah, they kind of mean walk in. . .we chose campsite B. Not labeled on the bluffy shore—once you find it, there is that sheer cliff to climb with all the camping gear. We chose to have our

Bluffs, Beaches, Lighthouses and Shipwrecks

"kitchen" on the rock shelf by our kayaks. For the evening we tied our kayaks on the rock shelf to a tree, but if there had been a summer storm, our kayaks would never have survived and would have been taken by the sea. Circumnavigating Rock Island by kayak would be much more difficult without kayaks. . .hence learn from our experience and reserve a numbered campsite on the sandy shoreline. Also, even though you reserved your campsite, you must stop at the camper registration station by the ferry dock on the southwestern shoreline by 3:00 pm, or your campsite could possibly be rebooked by someone else.

Once we climbed up to our campsite, it was covered by a beautiful canopy of white cedars, which made us nervous about mosquitoes, but lo and behold Rock Island doesn't generally have mosquitoes due to limited standing water! The rock in Rock Island is the Niagara escarpment popping up out of the lake and is made up of dolomite—sand and gravel deposited from glacial ice over 400 million years ago. This limestone like dolomite is a natural aquifer, allowing ground water to seep through the rock and down the vertical fractures on the shoreline bluffs. Our shade covers of white cedars love the dolomite rock with only the thin soil layer above it. These evergreen trees can grow to 50 feet tall and can live to over 700 years! Respect your elders and enjoy some of the oldest growth forest in the region. Look closely at the bark of the white cedars, when young the bark spirals to the left, and when they grow up to be adults after a century, the bark switches and starts to spiral to the right. While we relaxed after supper and played some cards, two deer and a fawn meandered through our campsite three feet from our tent gently foraging through, thank you kind visitors. Look also for coyote, muskrat, and perhaps a visiting bear.

The bluff top primitive lettered campsites are off the Thordarson Loop Trail which circles the entire outside of the island for a five mile plus hike. We took a pleasant stroll along the trail and met some of the other campers hiking in with their cartload of supplies and firewood—"are we close yet?" Which is more work, kayaking to our campsite or hiking to their campsite? Either way, the views are awesome! Rock Island offers almost ten miles of hiking trails leading to the famed Pottawatomie lighthouse, scenic overlooks, to the historic stone buildings, and down to the beach.

Want something more exciting as you relax by your camp fire? This is a perfect location to tell spooky tales in the glimmering light of the smoky wood fire. Rock Island is haunted. . .the campground is near the old Scandinavian settler's cemetery and an old Pottawatomi Native American village and cemetery…Owwweee. Voices, unusual noises, and flickering shapes have been seen over graves. Small ghostly children play around the graves. And the oldest lighthouse in the state, Rock Island's Pottawatomie lighthouse is supposedly haunted by its original lighthouse keeper, David Corbin who is buried on the island. Thumps in the night have been heard as he still checks his beloved lighthouse. . . Aaahhh. . .

We sleep quietly and peacefully under our green canopy with the wind rustling through the branches. The moon shines through the cedars creating interesting patterns against the tent walls. The Lake Michigan waves down below filter up to our tent and gradually lull us into pleasant dreams.

Morning comes, and off we start on our circle of this great Rock Island. Gentle waves lap along the shore for our launch as we round the bottom southeast corner of the island. We are awed by the beautiful white cliffs with crevasses, columns, and grottos, cascading with the deep forest green of the white cedars spotlighted by the pure blue sky. After only a mile, Rick pulls up to the rock shelf "I'm swimming", "but we just started", "I'm swimming, it's beautiful and the water is crystal clear, I'm swimming". "Okay dokey", and he's right, it is delightfully brisk and clean.

While swimming, we gaze north to Upper Michigan. Yup, Rock Island is the northernest point in Wisconsin of the Niagara Escarpment. From here the escarpment continues to bounce out of Lake Michigan to the "UP"—the Upper Peninsula of Michigan. It is a clear view six miles up to St Martin Island, the largest passage connecting Lake Michigan and Green Bay. St Martin Island is about the same size as Rock Island, and lucky for us is being acquired by the Nature Conservancy to become part of the Green Bay National Wildlife Refuge. St Martin Island, like Rock Island, has cobblestone beaches and rocky bluffs, topped with white cedar and hardwood forests. It is important for migrating dragonflies, bats, butterflies and Great Lake birds.

It also has an abandoned, one of a kind, hexagonal historic lighthouse.

We have often discussed hopscotching the Niagara Escarpment chain of islands from the Door County Peninsula to Washington Island, to Rock Island and kayaking north the six miles rounding St Martin Island. Two miles north of St Martin Island, keep on a going past the pin dot uninhabited islands of Gull, Little Gull and Gravely Islands. Hop another two and a half miles to Poverty Island. It is owned by the federal government and is a tree covered island with nothing but an abandoned lighthouse on the southern tip which is in disrepair. But. . . why, why is it called Poverty Island? There is a legend that there is a lost treasure chest of Civil War gold coins lost beneath the waves in a shipwreck. Or is the shipwreck Robert La Salle's long lost ship Le Griffen? The famous explorer searching for the passage to China and Japan built one of the first schooners to sail the Great Lakes. But on her maiden voyage, she departed Washington Island—and was never seen again. On our imaginary voyage, skim north another one mile to Summer Island, and finally you can land! The southern half of Summer Island is a Lake Superior State Forest (yes we know it is in Lake Michigan, do they?). From Summer Island it is just a mile

Kayak Wisconsin, Door County Peninsula

paddle to the Garden Peninsula tip of Upper Michigan. Whew! So it is quite possible to cruise from island to island in the Niagara Escarpment all the way up to the Garden Peninsula in the Upper Peninsula of Michigan.

Ah, another paddle for another day. Time to stop day dreaming and probing the horizon and hop back into our kayaks to resume our circumnavigation paddle. The entire east side of Rock Island escalates with lined bluffs, growing and shooting up to the sky. We coast on by a miniature bench, OK it just looks that way from down here, up above the cliff's scenic overlook. Come to the dramatic north point of Rock Island with it sheer imposing bluff casting its shadow down on us.

Way up on top of the bluff we can only see the ugly duckling lighthouse, just a steel skeleton tower with a solar panel light. The light tower is great protection for boats and ships, but disappointing to look at. But never fear! Slide your kayaks up on the rock shelf and take the steps provided up to the top of the bluff to be rewarded with the real treasure, the historic old lighthouse. This grand lady dates back to 1836 before Wisconsin was a state and was the first lighthouse to be built on Lake Michigan in Wisconsin. The original lighthouse built here was demolished in the 1850's and the one you can see today was constructed from the rock on the island with the lighthouse itself sitting on the northern gable. The light room is a nine sided lantern. The Pottawatomie Lighthouse was named after the Native Americans who lived in the area and Pottawatomie astutely means "keepers of the fire". Many hours of restoration have been put into this lighthouse and now in the summer, volunteer docents live in the lighthouse and will give you a free tour. After your tour, as you descend the stairs back to your kayaks, reflect on the difficulties of the lighthouse keepers. Steps like these were first built in 1879 as a convenience to obtain drinking water—that way they did not have hike the one mile south to the beach area for their drinking water and then carry it back up to the lighthouse.

Back in the boats, round the regal point and turn south along Rock Island's Green Bay side. The colossal cliffs continue more than a mile along the shoreline. Paddle slowly past the sheer cliffs as they jetty down to the water. Straight horizontal layers of rock build up over and over to the green cap tree line on top. Mini trees desperately attempt to get a strong hold in the vertical fissures in the rock face. Follow the bluffs as they dwindle to the southwest's serpents sandy tail.

Kayak Wisconsin, Door County Peninsula

Just when you thought this rock island was all about nature, the historical estate of the self made millionaire inventor Hjortur "Chester" Thoadarson slowly comes into view. The first attractive stone building is the guest house with the stone arch door, now Rock Island's ranger residence. Somewhere between the stone guest house and the ferry dock, pull up onto the shore to check out these incredible historic buildings. Next to the ferry dock is Mr. Thoadarson's vivid white dolomite Viking Hall Boathouse with its many arches. The upper level of Viking Hall has a large fireplace with Icelandic artist Halldor Elnarson's carvings along with some of the original twenty-four chairs with carved depictions of Nordic myths. Behind the giant casino hall, stand Mr. Thoadarson's Rock Island residence, the straight lined cobblestone building with the green roof which originally had a greenhouse attached to it. Thoadarson's greenhouse home is now used as the park shelter. Look for the estate gate, spring house, pantry, and the pagoda all in this area with their signature red tiled roofs. The water tower, which appears to never have been used for obtaining water, is actually located back on the southeast side of the island overlooking Lake Michigan. Chester Thoadarson died in 1945, and

Bluffs, Beaches, Lighthouses and Shipwrecks

his family sold the island to Wisconsin in1965 and since then has always been this stunning state park.

Ahh, we have completed circling all three sides of Rock Island's State Park's triangle. Time to return to your campsite, or follow that last tree that bravely lives on the shoal line that vainly attempts to connect to Washington Island and Jackson Harbor. Swing southeast to Old Camp Road if that is where you launched.

Logistics:

Directions to Jackson Harbor Ridges State Natural area public access:

45.3988, -86.8550. From Washington Island's ferry dock, turn north on Lobdell Point Road/County W, then turn north on Main Road (which happens to continue to be County Road W), driver 2.6 miles and turn east on Jackson Harbor Road (which interestingly enough continues to be County Road W) for 3.9 miles turning north and then again east to a parking area on the right side of the road. Carry in your kayaks about 200 feet to the shoreline. No restrooms, no fees.

Directions to Old Camp Road Washington Island public access:

45.3960, -86.8393. From Washington Island's ferry dock, turn north on Lobdell Point Rd/County Road W, then turn north on Main Road (which happens to continue to be County Road W) drive 2.6 miles, turn right on Jackson Harbor Road (which interestingly enough continues to be County Road W) for 3.5 miles, continue straight on Old Camp Road, at the T intersection turn left to stay on Old Camp Road, and then turn right to stay on Old Camp Road to Lake Michigan. No fee, no restrooms.

Directions to Rock Island State Park:

45.4090, -86.8292. The coordinates are for the ferry dock area which is considered the access point, but you may pull up your kayak on the south shore beach or on any rock shelf you feel comfortable. It's a state park, it's all public access!

Kayak Wisconsin, Door County Peninsula

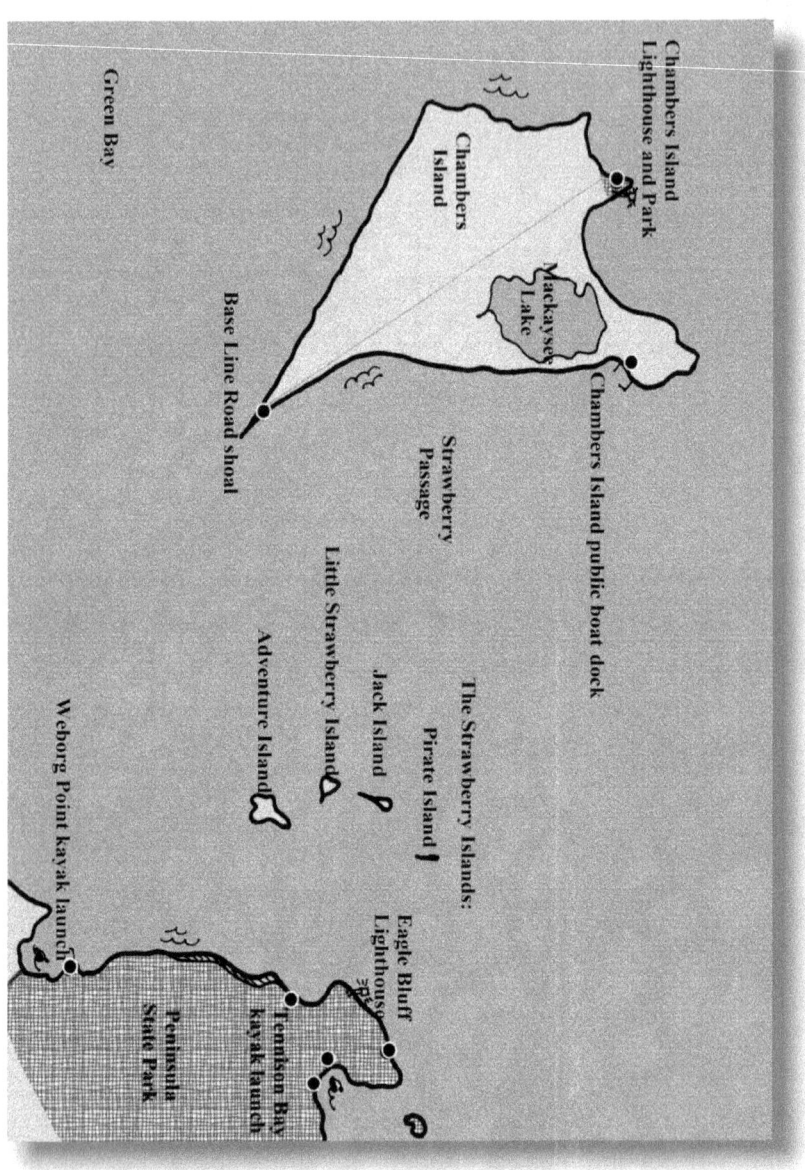

Bluffs, Beaches, Lighthouses and Shipwrecks

Bonus Island Paddle

Chambers and the Strawberry Islands

Peninsula State Park through the Strawberry Islands to Chambers Island
With Chambers Island lighthouse and an expansive view of the bluffs of Door County
12 miles

We love Chambers Island! We were greeted when we landed, and met the CIA. . .Chambers Island Association island folks. All warm, welcoming, and encouraging us to paddle back again. Oh, wait, we came for the vistas—which are incredibly memorable. Each of the private Strawberry Islands is unique, plus Chambers Island's sandy shoreline, and then the not to be missed view back to Door County Peninsula headlands: Deaths Door Bluff, Ellison Bluff, the Sister Bluffs, and Peninsula State Park's Eagle Point. Gotta' love it!

The shortest distance you could paddle to get to Chambers Island and back is 10 miles launching from Weborg Point in Peninsula State Park to the tip of Chambers Island's kite tail. But from the bottom tip of Chambers Island it would be a three and three quarter mile hike up Base Line Road to see the lighthouse and it would be a mistake to skip the lighthouse. To circumnavigate the island is an 18 mile paddle. Thus, we chose to launch at Peninsula State Park's Tennison Bay kayak launch, and weave through the Strawberry Islands to Chambers Island and back. Landing at the public boat dock on the eastern shoreline of the crossbars of Chambers Island's kite, we then strolled the 2 miles to the lighthouse. . .or at least that was our plan. . .but there is a story to be told…

Summers are so short. Finally got to tackle this island in early September, still a beautiful 74 degree day with light wind, or so it was predicted. Eyes on the water are worth ten predictions, and the wind was a wee bit more than expected and we had one to two foot plus whitecaps attacking from our port side. Slow progress as we paddled out of Tennison Bay and towards the islands. Looking from south to north we spy Adventure, Little Strawberry, Jack, and puny Pirate Island lined up jaggedly, all about one and a half miles off shore of Tennison Bay.

We wove between privately owned Adventure and Little Strawberry Islands. Adventure is the fattest strawberry of the Strawberry Islands, a whole half mile by a quarter mile, with a cobblestone base and a covering of green forest with several buildings poking out of the greenery. To our right, starboard, is Little Strawberry, the closest to an actual strawberry shape of the islands. Sweet Little Strawberry is the next largest at about a quarter mile by an eighth of a mile. She is looking quite green with only one home to blemish her. Why are they called Strawberry Islands you ask? Maybe by their shapes, but more likely they got thrown into the pail with Chambers Island which was famous for the lighthouse keeper's humungous red strawberry patch. And you thought Door County was famous only for cherries, shame on you.

Very little protection from the wind and waves from the small batch of strawberry islands, and now we head into Strawberry Passage between the Strawberry Islands and Chambers Island. This is a narrow, shallow channel and only schooners looking for harbor would attempt it. Today occasional motor boats and sailboats share the Strawberry passage with us, except for the pelicans. They allowed us to paddle close enough to see their long pinkish bills with the orange yellow pouch below and the yellow circle around their black eyes. They were floating and fishing for some of the three pounds of fish they like to eat each day. Must have decided we were getting close enough, as they lifted their sixteen pound bodies up and flapped away showing off their nine foot wingspan with the black outer feathers. Pelicans fly in a tucked neck Z shaped posture that is helpful to distinguish them from the other large birds.

Also joining us on our four mile passage across the Strawberry Passage was a couple of monarchs floating along on the breeze. Their bright orange wings with black veins and white dots on the edges are striking against the indigo blue water and paler shade of blue sky. We were best pals together for a few moments. Perhaps the monarchs were deciding if the kayaks were a really large sunflower or a safe place for a short rest, as both the pelicans and the monarchs shall soon be migrating back south to Mexico and the gulf coast states.

Appreciate the pleasant winged company to paddle with across the channel as the white caps finally start settling down and we enjoy the calming lee of Chambers Island. As we sail our tiny ships towards the island we evoke the memory of 1816 when four large schooners sailed past here too. They were the first sailing vessels in the bay since Robert LaSalle lost his Le Griffen schooner in Death's Door in 1689—literally as she has never been found. The 1816 schooners were commanded by Colonel Talbot Chambers on his way to establish a military post in present day city of Green Bay. He apparently liked the island and named it after himself, a little presumptuous don't ya think? He also named Washington Island after the flagship of his fleet.

Chambers Island is much larger than all four of the strawberry islands put together. The island is shaped like a diamond kite with the bottom of the longeron spine in the southeast corner running almost four miles northwest up Base Line Road to Gibraltar Park and the lighthouse. The cross spar runs about three miles in a southwest to northeast direction. There is a "hole" in the kite. . . Mackaysee Lake is a 347 acre lake on the northeast side of the island.

The island is almost smack dab in the middle of Green Bay, six miles from the Door County Peninsula and seven miles to Upper Michigan, fifty miles from the base of Green Bay and thirty

Kayak Wisconsin, Door County Peninsula

six miles to the top of Rock Island and Wisconsin's water border with Michigan. And we are almost there. We are aiming for just north of the isthmus between Mackaysee Lake and Green Bay at the northeast tip where we can see the rock harbor wall protruding out into the bay.

We land on the shoreline by the public dock. We finally turn around and are awed by the view of where we've come from—the marvelous sea cliff coast line of Door County's peninsula. Wow! Directly across is Peninsula State Park's Eagle Bluff rising above the Strawberry Islands, then a little north are the twin Sister Bluffs, next Ellison Bluff juts up and out, and finally distinctive Deathsdoor Bluff. Spectacular!

Time to stretch! Time for lunch, kind 'a hungry for strawberries. . .wonder why. . . Well that would have been a superb snack, but we brought Door County very tasty cherry salsa instead. After lunch, we are greeted by our first islanders. Cheerfully helpful, they offer other beautiful sandy beach landings such as at the base of Base Line Road, Chambers Island's kite tail as it spits out to Hanover Shoal.

We are ready to stroll over to see the lighthouse. "It's simple. There are only two basic roads, Island Drive and Base Line Road". "Hmm, what's this road?" "Is it this one or that one?" By luck, right then, a van drove by (can't be too many of those considering there is no public car ferry. . .). We politely ask for directions, and are promptly invited into the van. "We'll take you there". Gerry, from Classic Boat Tours of Door County, has motored over to Chambers Island, a bit faster than our technique, and is providing a tour of Chambers Island. The smiling troupe allows a few vagabonds to join their expedition.

First stop is a view of Lake Mackaysee, the "hole" in Chamber's Island kite shape. There are actually two islands in the lake, in the island, in the lake. Got that? Lake Mackaysee takes up almost one eighth of the entire island and is a notable fishin' hole for bass, pike, perch, bluegill, and even sturgeon. Nearby, our adopted tour guide shows us a Native American artifact, carvings on a stone, and explains that archeologists have also discovered burial mounds on the island.

Up we go on Island Drive past the airport. Are ya' kiddin' me? Honestly! There is a grassy airstrip, and we can attest to actual airplanes on the strip. Never considered flying over to the island. . . bet it is a bit faster. . .

We curve around North Bay and get a fantastic view across Green Bay to the state of Michigan's

Kayak Wisconsin, Door County Peninsula

Upper Peninsula. Wave to the Uppers! Now get the pronunciation correct, it is "U-pers" not "uppers". Not only do we have a great lookout, but if we were still kayaking, it would only be about one mile paddling west to be in Upper Michigan water territory. That means this is the only place you can paddle west to get into an eastern time zone. See, we listened to our teacher.

We turn right onto Base Line Road. . .oh look, there truly are homemade road signs with arrows pointing the way to the lighthouse, we just were not very observant. . .maybe we were hoping for a ride? The lighthouse is located at Gibraltar Park on the middle tip of the northern side of the island. This is the origin of Base Line Road, a straight as an arrow lane, heading directly down to the bottom tip at Hanover Shoal. This is not by accident. It was one of the jobs of the lighthouse keeper to keep this road open and wide so that ships in Strawberry Channel could see this lighthouse lantern on the other side of the island.

Here we meet Mary Ann and Joel, volunteer caretakers of the lighthouse for the past thirty eight, count them, thirty eight years—absolutely amazing, what dedication. And true to island tradition, so happy to show us their summer home of Chambers Island Lighthouse.

Bluffs, Beaches, Lighthouses and Shipwrecks

Chambers Island Lighthouse was built in 1868, the same year as Eagle Bluff Lighthouse in Peninsula State Park. Both are one and a half stories and both are built of cream colored bricks from Milwaukee. Whereas, the Eagle Bluff lighthouse has a square lantern tower, Chambers Island lantern tower is a more unique octagonal shape. We were able to climb the fifty-five cast iron steps to the top of the tower and relish the view towards Upper Michigan at an even better advantage. The ten sided decagonal medium sized fourth order Fresnel lens had a different flashing pattern than Eagle Bluff's to help mariners tell the difference. The Fresnel lens lantern was removed in 1958 but an automated light is nearby to protect captains, crew and recreational enthusiasts.

The lighthouse is one of three Door County Lighthouses considered haunted by the old, original, and longest lasting lighthouse keeper, Lewis Williams. Heavy footsteps have been heard coming down those beautiful cast-iron circular steps and his footsteps creaks through the home and ends with a click of the door. Tools have disappeared and end up in unlikely places, beds even shake. Eeeewww. . .we were too chicken to ask Mary Ann or Joel if they've had ghostly encounters. . .

Kayak Wisconsin, Door County Peninsula

Most in depth historical and intimate lighthouse island tour ever, but our favorite part? The wooden outhouse—it is an appreciated necessity and a flush toilet. Except that is not what makes this outhouse so special. Mary and Joel have added a little library with share a book policy. On the shelf was the "1000 places to see before you die" book, an entertaining read, but we think we should sneak in a page about friendly Chambers Island.

We hitchhiked our way back to the boat dock with Classic Gerry and his merry band of tourists. After hugs to Gerry and Mary, our new pals, we don our PFD's (personal floatation devices) and kayak skirts. We race Gerry and his outboard boat back across the Strawberry Passage. OK, he won, not much of a race, he left us in his wake in the first fifty feet.

Has the wind died down or does the quiet lee extend all the way to the Strawberry Isle's now? The cool thing is that we have that magnificent panorama the whole paddle back. Far away north is Deathsdoor Bluff looking like a jet crashing into the bay with its two tiered cliff. Giant Ellison Bluff is next followed by the close knit Sister Bluffs, and then our destination, Eagle Bluff soaring above Jack and Pirate Islands.

Bluffs, Beaches, Lighthouses and Shipwrecks

Now there is no way you could call Jack Island strawberry shaped. He is aptly named as he looks like a male amoeba with his tail vainly trying to mate with sweet Little Strawberry Island with a submarine attack as his tail trails under the water. Little Strawberry repels his advances quite properly with wild wave action over Jack's underwater tail. Jack Island is a cobble stone base and Jack's top of trees has a manly crew cut giving way to a grassy plain.

We pass by Jack Island's north side and give a glance to Pirate Island which looks like a white string dropped into the sea of azure blue, with a couple of poplars valiantly growing along the ridge line. No pirate could ever find a place to hide out on Pirate Island, and no pirate stranded on the island would survive long, without even a coconut to talk to. But that shouldn't stop us from putting on our eye patch, arg, hoisting up our black flag, and singing "yo ho ho and a. . ." in our best pirate accent!

Heave ho, in we go, into Tennison Bay. Nice view of Eagle Bluff lighthouse, Chamber Island's copycat sister, both grand old dames.

Land ho, the tired pirates land ashore in our brightly colored mini pirate ships. Grateful to our new found friends, the CIA—"Cheerful Island Folks", Chamber Island Association representatives.

Logistics:

Directions to Tennison Bay Canoe/Kayak launch at Peninsula State Park:

45.1619, -87.2350. Enter the park off of Highway 42 at State Park Road which turns into Shore Road. Take a left and continue on Shore Road where it meets with Bluff Road. The kayak launch ramp is in the Tennison Bay Campground– turn left to the ramp by the shore.

Directions to Weborg Point kayak launch at Peninsula State Park (alternate launch site):

45.1339, -87.2404. Enter the park off of Highway 42 at State Park Road by Fish Creek which turns into Shore Road. Follow Shore Road for less than 1 mile to Weborg Point parking area. Shower and restrooms available.

Bluffs, Beaches, Lighthouses and Shipwrecks

Directions to Chambers Island Gibraltar Park and lighthouse:

45.2021, -87.3659. The park is located on the north side of Chambers Island. From Tennison Bay kayak launch in Peninsula State Park paddle towards the south tip of Chambers Island up and around the south side to the lighthouse property. The paddle is about 9.7 miles.

Directions to Chambers Island public boat dock:

45.2030, -87.3359. The public boat dock is located on northeast tip of Chambers Island. From Tennison Bay kayak launch in Peninsula State Park paddle 5.7 miles through the Strawberry Islands toward the northeast tip of Chambers Island to the rock harbor wall of the private marina. The boat dock is at the southern side of the marina.

Directions to Chambers Island Base Line Road at the southern tip of the island:

45.1580, -87.3284. Base Line Road ends at the southern tip of Chambers Island. From Tennison

Kayak Wisconsin, Door County Peninsula

Bay kayak launch in Peninsula State Park paddle 4.6 miles through the Strawberry Islands to the southern tip of Chambers Island.

Don't want to paddle? Other access to Chambers Island:

Classic Boat Tours of Door County: http://www.classicboattours.com

And always end with a paddle lift!

Thank you for reading my book. If you enjoyed it, won't you please take a moment to leave me a review at your favorite retailer?

Thanks!

Babs Smith

About the Author

Babs Malchow Smith

Babs has an easy propensity to saying yes to just about any adventure one of her brothers dreams up. She is married to her husband, Mike, who indulges and lets her West wind flow, whereas, he steers clear and likes to stay well grounded. Babs is an occupational therapist by trade, so although she is not the most skillful paddler, she is handy at the end of the day when any tendonitis muscle ache flares up.

Connect with me:

Chat with me at my e-mail:
babs_daykayaking@yahoo.com

Kayak Wisconsin, Door County Peninsula

Special Thanks

Paddling Buddies

Rick and Chris Malchow

My brother Rick is the true adventurer. He researches and plans our trips. He is our fearless leader, giving us a gentle push off when launching, and guides us safely into shore in rough terrain. Rick is also our camp chef, and we eat very well with no trace of traditional camp fare. He is a powerful dynamic paddler who can outdistance us at any time.

My sister-in-law Chris, with her easy laugh, helps Rick from overstressing on the packing details. She is the organizer who always seems to know the answer to "where's the. . .?" Chris is a great cook in her own right who takes over the chef position at home base. She is a natural paddler with a smooth, easy, efficient stroke.

Graphic Design

Ryan Malchow

Ryan, Rick and Chris's son, has a B.A. in Marketing and Visual Arts, which is a great asset to me, his aunt Babs. He's an artist who enjoys creative pursuits of painting and photography, as well as fish keeping, and the family love of disc golf.

Mark Malco

Mark is the original kayaker in the family. His enthusiasm has spread like a Mississippi flood throughout the siblings. Mark is a detail oriented kayaker who enjoys the thrill of the coastline of his Pacific Northwest.

Editing

Gerry La Bonte

Gerry and his wife Ann are great friends who love sailing and canoeing, but are learning to love kayaking and shipwreck searching. Thanks for teaching me what an ellipses and em-dash is.

www.ingramcontent.com/pod-product-compliance
Lightning Source LLC
Chambersburg PA
CBHW060455090426
42735CB00011B/1995